MW00914100

M W
& R

OTTAWA WITH KIDS
The Complete Family Travel Guide to Attractions, Sites and Events in Ottawa

JAMES HALE & JOANNE MILNER

MACFARLANE WALTER & ROSS
TORONTO

Macfarlane Walter & Ross
37A Hazelton Avenue
Toronto, Canada M5R 2E3

Canadian Cataloguing in Publication Data

Hale, James, 1954-
    Ottawa with kids

Includes index.
ISBN 0–921912–98–6

1. Ottawa (Ont.) – Guidebooks.
2. Family recreation – Ontario – Ottawa – Guidebooks.
3. Children – Travel – Ontario – Ottawa – Guidebooks.
I. Milner, J. (Joanne), 1950 –
II. Title.

FC3096.18.H3   1996   917.13'84044'083   C96-930906–6
F1059.5.09H3   1996

The publisher gratefully acknowledges the support of the Canada Council and the Ontario Arts Council

Printed and bound in Canada

To our parents —

for always taking us along for the ride.

Acknowledgments

Good researchers are hard to find, and we've been lucky to benefit from more than a dozen years of terrific feedback from our kids — Sabrina and Jessi — who have always been eager to explore their hometown.

Our thanks to Jan Walter of Macfarlane Walter & Ross for her encouragement and advice, and to Barbara Czarnecki for her unflagging attention to detail.

We would also like to thank Jennifer Hagen of the Ottawa Tourism & Convention Authority and Guy Thériault of Parks Canada, who shared their extensive contacts with us.

James also extends his thanks to Lynda Leonard, Phil Jenkins, and Martha Nelson for their enthusiasm and support.

Growing up in Ottawa, it's easy to take the region's beauty for granted. This book has helped us see it through new eyes. On behalf of everyone who enjoys the riches Ottawa offers, we would like to acknowledge Jacques Gréber, Douglas Fullerton, Charlotte Whitton, Don Reid, Marion Dewar, Jean Pigott, and everyone else who had a hand in shaping the face of this city.

Contents

Introduction

We took our first extended trip with our two children, Sabrina and Jessi, seven years ago when they were six and four. Our destination was Prince Edward Island, and we set out determined not to repeat the experience of travelling with our own parents years earlier. Both of us recall seemingly endless car trips without an idea of where we were being taken, or what we were going to do when — if ever — we got there.

Even with that determination, however, there were problems. One of our favourite family stories recounts the time one of the kids informed a restaurant full of people that her hamburger tasted "like dog food." Perhaps that was because we had chosen a seafood restaurant without bothering to check ahead to see if they served anything else a child might like.

It's little reminders like that experience that keep us honest when planning a vacation that involves the children. You can never underestimate the difference that planning can make between a disaster and the trip of a lifetime. And you can't always count on what tourist brochures tell you; an advertising copywriter's idea of family fun can be your child's version of unrelieved boredom.

We were both born and raised in Ottawa, a rarity in a city that has traditionally had a large transient population. The service industry in this fully bilingual city attracts a large number of young francophones who speak English as a second language. Young people who want to work for the federal government come to Ottawa from across the country; people raised here who don't want to be civil servants often have to seek their fortune elsewhere.

When our girls were young, we lived in a downtown neighbourhood and learned what features in the city attracted their attention, and what museums and shops were geared to their interests. Now that we live in a small village outside Ottawa, we've come to know the city all over again, the way visitors see it.

Although *Ottawa with Kids* has been written with the tourist family in mind, it is not aimed at visitors exclusively. Two characteristics of the city give it a broader scope: many Ottawa residents, especially those with young children, weren't born here; and most Ottawa families live in one of the 14 communities that collectively form the National Capital Region, well outside the core. If you call Ottawa home but you're not familiar with all the historical sites of the city, the festivals, the parks, and the shops that cater especially to children, we hope your family will find *Ottawa with Kids* helpful in discovering the nation's capital.

Unlike other guidebooks, *Ottawa with Kids* looks at the city through the eyes of parents travelling with children, from infants to teenagers. Its aim is to give you a realistic idea of what you can expect, as well as to point out some of the lesser-known destinations — the ones that most tourists never see.

A book like this is an organic thing, just like a city itself. Events change, restaurants open and existing ones change their menus, new services enter the marketplace. We welcome your suggestions for future editions of *Ottawa with Kids* — recommendations, corrections, or criticisms. Kindly address them to James Hale and Joanne Milner, c/o Macfarlane Walter & Ross, 37A Hazelton Avenue, Toronto ON M5R 2E3.

Have a terrific time showing your kids Canada's capital city.

James Hale and Joanne Milner

How to use Ottawa with Kids

The cardinal rule when travelling in any city with kids is: **Call first**. We've tried to provide phone numbers for every destination and service listed in *Ottawa with Kids*, and we encourage you to phone ahead to ensure that the hours haven't changed, or that something hasn't been cancelled. The disappointment of what appears to a child as a broken promise can ruin your entire trip.

• The National Capital Region has two area codes. All the museums, businesses, and services resident in Ontario use the 613 area code, while those across the Ottawa River in west Quebec use 819. All telephone numbers listed in *Ottawa with Kids* are 613 numbers unless otherwise specified.

• We've included our best guess at how long a visit or event will take you, allowing time for a snack break or a quick lunch. Your actual time may vary, of course, depending on the ages of your children and their interests and attention spans. Chapter 1 has some sample itineraries to suggest how much you can expect to fit into your time in Ottawa.

• Throughout the book, we've indicated attractions or events that best combine value for money, originality, and family orientation. These are Ottawa services or institutions that have consistently proven themselves with our children and other families we've consulted. To them, we award the teddy bear symbol 🧸 of kid satisfaction.

• Budget is always a concern when travelling with a family, and we've included prices wherever possible. Many attractions in this most tourist-conscious of cities have special family rates (usually defined as two adults and two children), and many offer free admission to preschoolers. The prices listed were accurate at press time, but some changes are inevitable; always call ahead to confirm prices.

Ottawa and Area

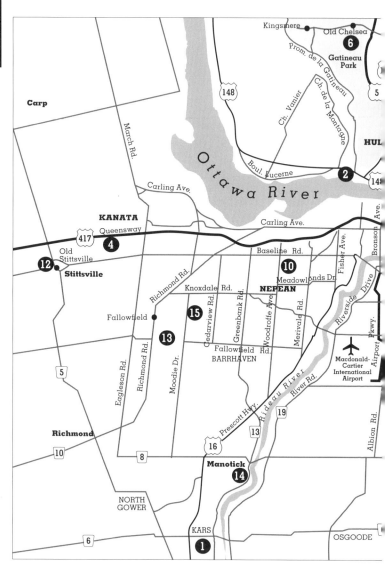

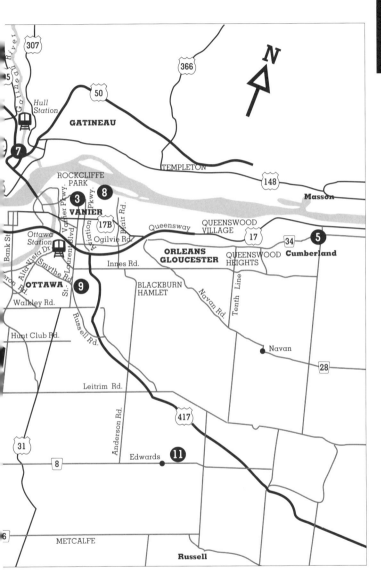

9. National Museum of
   Science and Technology
10. Nepean Museum
11. Patterson's Berry Farm
12. Stittsville Flea Market

13. Valleyview Little
    Animal Farm
14. Watson's Mill
15. Wild Bird Care Centre

3

Central Ottawa

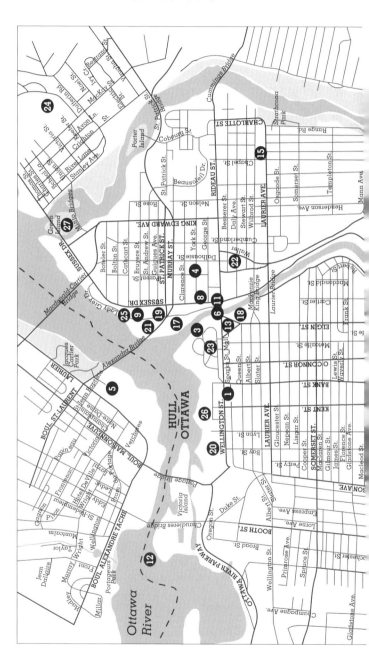

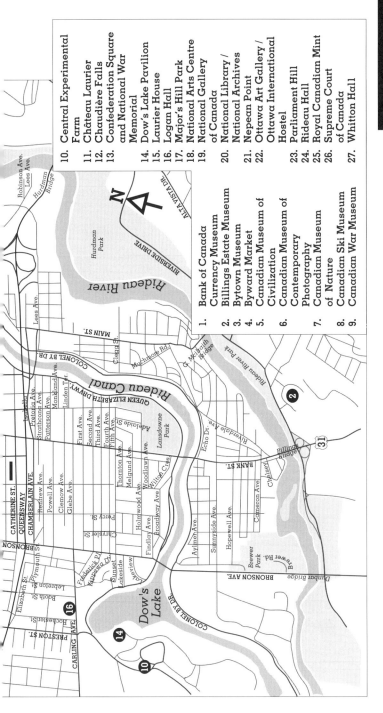

10. Central Experimental Farm
11. Château Laurier
12. Chaudière Falls
13. Confederation Square and National War Memorial
14. Dow's Lake Pavilion
15. Laurier House
16. Logan Hall
17. Major's Hill Park
18. National Arts Centre
19. National Gallery of Canada
20. National Library / National Archives
21. Nepean Point
22. Ottawa Art Gallery / Ottawa International Hostel
23. Parliament Hill
24. Rideau Hall
25. Royal Canadian Mint
26. Supreme Court of Canada
27. Whitton Hall

1. Bank of Canada Currency Museum
2. Billings Estate Museum
3. Bytown Museum
4. Byward Market
5. Canadian Museum of Civilization
6. Canadian Museum of Contemporary Photography
7. Canadian Museum of Nature
8. Canadian Ski Museum
9. Canadian War Museum

1: Planning your trip to Ottawa

There's little chance for kids to be bored in Ottawa. In addition to being home to a number of Canada's major historical, cultural, and scientific institutions, it is a city of great natural beauty — whether the countryside is rich and verdant, or covered in knee-deep snow. Ottawa is truly a year-round destination. Winterlude, the annual festival of ice and snow, is a major tourist draw, just like the Canadian Tulip Festival and the summertime's Cultures Canada.

Ottawa's other significant feature is its proximity to rural surroundings. You can be on top of a ski hill at 2 pm, and enjoying hot chocolate in a downtown bistro at 2:30. In warm weather, 30 minutes by car will take you to a sandy beach in the middle of a conservation area. The choice — town or country, indoors or outdoors — is up to you.

Climate: a question of extremes

One good thing you can say about Ottawa's weather is that there's never any doubt which season it is. You can count on hot, humid, sunny days at the peak of summer, and frigid temperatures with plenty of snow in the dead of winter. On warm spring days it some-times seems you can hear the

Ice sculpture at the annual Winterlude festival

flowers pushing up through the thawing earth, and in fall the trees are ablaze with colour.

So how hot and how cold does it get? The average daily temperature in July is 21 degrees Celsius (70 degrees Fahrenheit); for January it's -11 degrees Celsius (12 degrees Fahrenheit). But it's not unusual to experience temperatures in the vicinity of 30 degrees Celsius (86 degrees Fahrenheit) in mid-July. On the other end of the scale, the temperature can plunge to -30 degrees Celsius (-26 degrees Fahrenheit) in late January.

But those temperature extremes don't tell the entire story. The high humidity can add what feels like an extra 10 degrees to the actual temperature. In winter, a stiff north wind can push the windchill into the range where exposed flesh can be harmed after just a few minutes. Still, for every day when it's unwise to stray far from your air-conditioner or your cosy hotel cocoon, there are dozens when outdoor activities can be fun and healthy if you're dressed properly.

Warm raingear for your children is a must if you visit in March or November, usually the wettest months, and warm coats, boots, hats, scarves, and mittens are a necessity if you are arriving in time for Winterlude in February. For the Canadian Tulip Festival in

Short-stay itineraries

Planning a short stay in any city can be a challenge, especially if the members of your family have diverse interests. Fortunately, Ottawa's compact scale makes it convenient to combine a range of activities without a lot of travelling across the city. The following short-stay itineraries offer combinations of activities that are convenient, cost little, and have something for everyone in your family. Check the site listings for specific hours and admission fees, if any. All the itineraries assume that you are starting from downtown Ottawa.

2-day itineraries
Spring/summer/ early fall

DAY 1 Morning: Watch the Changing the Guard ceremony on Parliament Hill (weather permitting, mid-June to late August only) and tour the Parliament Buildings.

Afternoon: Walk through the Byward Market, taking time out for lunch; then head across the Alexandra Bridge to the Canadian Museum of Civilization.

DAY 2 Morning: Pack a picnic lunch and board one of the Piccadilly Bus Tours double-deckers at Confederation Square. Get off the bus at the Central Experimental Farm, visit the animals, and enjoy a picnic at the Dominion Arboretum.

Afternoon: Board another bus and finish your tour. Visit the Canadian War Museum.

Late fall/winter

DAY 1 Morning: Visit the National Gallery of Canada.

Afternoon: Head for a skate down the Rideau Canal, stopping for beaver-tails midway through your loop.

DAY 2 Morning: Enjoy the scenery of Gatineau Park from the cross-country ski trails.

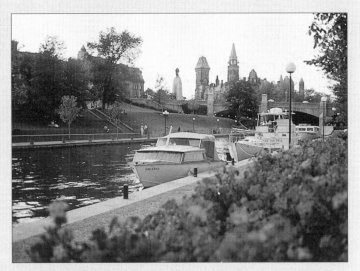

Mooring in the city centre on the Rideau Canal

Afternoon: Warm up at the Canadian Museum of Nature.

4-day itineraries

Add the following attractions to the two-day itineraries.

Spring/summer/early fall

DAY 3 Morning: Rent some bikes behind the Château Laurier and head out for a bicycle tour of either Westboro or New Edinburgh.

Afternoon: Rest your legs on a boat tour of the Ottawa section of the Rideau Canal.

DAY 4: Drive into the Gatineau Hills for a visit to the Mackenzie King Estate. From here it's a short drive to historic old Wakefield (full day).

Late fall/winter

DAY 3 Morning: Head out to the National Museum of Science and Technology. Don't forget your skates.

Afternoon: Make your way to the Dow's Lake Pavilion and skate back downtown.

DAY 4: Make a day of it at the Canadian Museum of Civilization, including crafts at the Children's Museum and an eye-popping IMAX or OMNIMAX film.

9

May or the Gatineau Hot Air Balloon Festival in September, you should include some windbreakers and an umbrella or two, just in case. You can hear an updated weather forecast by dialling 998-3439.

Where to get more information

Ottawa has two year-round visitor information centres in the downtown core. In high season a kiosk called **Info Ottawa**, at 101 Sparks Street, offers tickets and brochures.

• **Canada's Capital Information Centre:**
14 Metcalfe Street,
1-800-465-1867 or 239-5000
Operated by the National Capital Commission, the centre is open Victoria Day to Labour Day daily 8:30 am–9 pm; Labour Day to Victoria Day, Mondays–Saturdays 9 am–5 pm, Sundays 10 am–4 pm. Visitors can obtain information on various events in the region using touch-screens or computer printouts. A wide selection of brochures and maps is also on hand. One hour of free parking is available at the World Exchange Plaza on Metcalfe Street,

Ottawa on-line

If you have access to the Internet, you can take a virtual tour of the capital at *http://www.iatech.com/tour/*. For digitized photographs of the region, see *http://www.scs.carleton.ca/ottawa/ottawa.html*. Both sites offer links to others that are related to activities in Ottawa and environs. Several museums and facilities have their own home pages: look for an Internet address in the listings.

between Albert and Queen Streets. Bring your parking voucher to the information centre for validation.

• **Ottawa Tourism and Convention Authority Visitor Information Centre:**
65 Elgin Street, 237-5158
Open May 1 to Labour Day daily 9 am–9 pm; Labour Day to April 30, Mondays–Saturdays 9 am–5 pm, Sundays 10 am–4 pm. Located inside the National Arts Centre (NAC) on Confederation Square, the centre offers brochures and tourist maps, as well as a

Parliament Hill

touch-screen terminal. Visitors can park free for 30 minutes in the NAC garage (enter from Elgin Street). Bring your parking voucher to the information centre for validation.

Newspapers, magazines, and guides

It's impossible for a book like *Ottawa with Kids* to cover all the new or one-time events, special programs, art exhibits, and concerts that are staged in the city throughout the year. Pick up some of these publications for up-to-date information on activities for families in the city.

- **The Ottawa Citizen:** Eastern Ontario's largest daily newspaper publishes a daily calendar of events, as well as features on upcoming attractions. Available at newsstands, street boxes, and convenience stores, and by subscription. Call 596-1950.
- **Ottawa Magazine:** A monthly magazine with a regular calendar of events and occasional features of interest to parents in the city. Available at newsstands or by subscription. Call 234-7751.
- **Ottawa Parent:** A free monthly tabloid newspaper

with articles of interest to parents, events listings, and columns on healthy eating, childcare, and family entertainment. Available at shopping centres, grocery stores, and children's retailers, and by subscription. Call 721-0811.

- **The Ottawa Sun:** Ottawa's morning tabloid has regular features on family activities, along with events listings and advertisements. Available at newsstands, street boxes, and convenience stores, and by subscription. Call 739-7200.
- **Ottawa Visitor Guide:** An annual publication of the Ottawa Tourism and Convention Authority with comprehensive listings of events and attractions. Available at Ottawa's two visitor information centres. Call 241-7888.
- **Ottawa Xpress:** An alternative weekly tabloid that covers entertainment, politics, and social issues of concern to teenagers and young adults. Available every Thursday at newsstands, music stores, theatres, and bookstores, or by subscription. Call 237-8226.
- **Where: Ottawa-Hull:** A free monthly magazine with extensive listings of events, restaurants, and shops. Available in hotel rooms, tourist information offices, and public buildings, and by subscription. Call 241-7888.

The National War Memorial, with the Château Laurier's turrets and spires

Happy holidays

Tourists unfamiliar with Canada should be aware of several holidays.

- **Victoria Day:** The third Monday in May, and the day Canadians declare summer. In Ottawa, stores in tourist areas like the Byward Market and restaurants are usually the only businesses that remain open. In Hull, most stores are open, but all banks and liquor stores are closed.
- **Canada Day:** July 1. Convenience stores and restaurants are usually open, although often with reduced hours.
- **Civic Holiday:** The first Monday in August. In Ottawa, stores in tourist areas like the Byward Market and restaurants are usually the only businesses that remain open. In Hull, most stores are open.
- **Thanksgiving Day:** The second Monday in October. Some stores in tourist areas and restaurants are usually open, although with reduced hours.
- **Remembrance Day:** November 11. Many stores remain closed until noon.

2: From Bytown to Ottawa: a capital tale

In many ways, the history of Ottawa mirrors the fairy tale of the ugly duckling. Founded as a rough, backcountry lumbering town, it has been transformed over the years into a beautiful, if small, national capital filled with historic sites and cultural showplaces. Like the swan that emerged from the ugly duckling, Ottawa had the right natural ingredients to grow into a beauty. The region has striking geography, created by the junction of the Ottawa, Gatineau, and Rideau Rivers, the heavily treed Gatineau Hills north of the Ottawa, and the rich pastureland to the west and south.

As a largely navigable water route between the St. Lawrence River and the many lakes in the region south of Georgian Bay, the Ottawa River was used for thousands of years by aboriginal hunters and trappers. Evidence of settlements of the Algonquian people has been found up and down what is known today as the Ottawa Valley.

The wide mouth of the Ottawa — today's Lake of Two Mountains, near Montreal — was an invitation that French explorer Samuel de Champlain couldn't ignore. In 1613, he followed the river north until he reached the junction of two other rivers (now called the Rideau and the Gatineau). Legend has it that Champlain mounted the rocky cliffs on the south bank of the Ottawa, near the present site of the

A depiction of 18th-century Algonquian Indians on the Ottawa River

Parliament Buildings, to take his bearings from the stars, and lost his astrolabe there.

Champlain's journals drew European traders to the Ottawa River for the next 150 years, but it wasn't until 1800 that Philemon Wright, a United Empire Loyalist from Massachusetts, recognized the economic potential of the region's lumber. He built a sawmill on the river opposite from where Champlain had camped and named his settlement Wrightsville (now Hull).

Events developed quickly over the following decades. The catalyst was the War of 1812. After the United

States attacked Canada, Britain's only remaining North American colony, the

Samuel de Champlain's statue, Major's Hill Park

Canada's European roots

The Vikings were the first white people to land on the shores of what is now Canada, possibly as early as the ninth century, but it wasn't until French explorer Jacques Cartier arrived in 1535 that word of the new land spread to Europe. The name Canada, derived from the Huron-Iroquois word *kanata* meaning village or settlement, was given to the lands along the St. Lawrence River. Inland exploration and settlement by Europeans began to flourish after Samuel de Champlain published his diaries of his travels north up the Ottawa River. In the 1600s France laid claim to massive holdings that ran from Hudson's Bay in the north to the Gulf of Mexico in the south.

Britain gained its first foothold on the new land in 1713, when the Treaty of Utrecht gave it large parts of what is today Atlantic Canada. Forty years later, the British were challenging the French for more territory inland. The turning point — and the event that still defines relations between francophones and anglophones in Canada — came at the French stronghold of Quebec City. In September 1759, British troops led by James Wolfe defeated the Marquis de Montcalm's garrison on the Plains of Abraham, and Britain took over all of North America, from the Arctic to the Mexican border. Very quickly, the British established their domination by building their control over the French colony's business and finance sectors. But the American Revolution reduced the British sphere of influence once again to the northern half of the continent.

On July 1, 1867, the British Parliament made Canada an independent country within the British Empire. At the time of Confederation, the new Dominion of Canada included Ontario, Quebec, Nova Scotia, and New Brunswick. A parliamentary government, modelled on the British system, was established at Ottawa with Sir John A. Macdonald as its first prime minister. Over the 1870s the country expanded westward to the Rocky Mountains and the Pacific, north to the Arctic Ocean, and east to embrace Prince Edward Island. In 1949 Newfoundland & Labrador joined the federation, now made up of ten provinces and two territories.

Canada remained very much under Britain's influence until World War I. On Easter Sunday, 1917, Canadian troops led an attack on Vimy Ridge, a stubbornly defended hill near Arras, France. More than 3,500 Canadians were killed in the victorious attack, an action that was credited with helping turn the tide in the war. Latter-day historians consider that Canada gained its nationhood on Vimy Ridge. Today Canada is a member of the Commonwealth, with Queen Elizabeth II as its head of state, but it has developed a social, political, and artistic culture all its own.

Canada's political history in the second half of the 20th century has been dominated by tension between Quebec and the rest of the country. The 1960s saw a rise of Quebec nationalism, including a brief phase of urban terrorism marked by mailbox bombings and kidnappings. In 1980 and 1995, nationalist forces led unsuccessful attempts to win support from Quebec residents to form a separate nation. Canada's close ties to its British heritage continue to rankle with those who see Quebec as a distinct culture.

Bilingualism has been a national policy since 1969, and nowhere is it more widely practised than in Ottawa. The federal government operates in both French and English. Most signs and all tourist literature are in both languages, and many businesses in the region offer bilingual service.

Lieutenant-Colonel John By

British determined that the St. Lawrence River was too vulnerable to invading forces. Lieutenant-Colonel John By of the Royal Engineers was assigned to construct an alternative supply route — a canal between the Wrightsville site and the eastern tip of Lake Ontario. In 1826, By established a campsite on the bluffs across the Ottawa from Wrightsville. The canal project demanded a large corps of labourers, as well as merchants to serve their needs, so over the next two years Bytown, as it had been dubbed, grew like Topsy. The sloping topography of the nascent town created a natural split between Upper Town and Lower Town —west and east — with By's English officers and the richer merchants living on the higher ground while the French and Irish labourers and their rough taverns occupied the land at the foot of the bluffs.

In addition to overseeing construction of the canal, By also laid out a grid of streets for his settlement, which by 1850 was a thriving lumbering town. Using power produced by the Chaudière Falls and Rideau Falls, several mills produced lumber for the hungry market in the United States. On January 1, 1855, Bytown achieved city status, and the name Ottawa (an English translation of the Algonquian term for traders) was bestowed on it.

There's a myth that Queen Victoria chose Ottawa as the capital of Canada by pointing her finger blindly at a map. The truth is far more prosaic. The rough-and-tumble city was chosen to settle a rivalry between other burgeoning cities, including Montreal, Toronto, and Kingston. The queen's choice was made public on New Year's Eve, 1857.

By's canal ended at the mouth of the Rideau River;
the future site of the Parliament Buildings rises on the right

Her choice may have been politically expedient, but the thought of being sent to Ottawa must have horrified the lawyers, physicians, and wealthy merchants who sought political power. Ottawa's image had been fixed in the public mind by an event in 1849. Tension between the gentry of Upper Town and the workers of Lower Town had erupted in a riot in Lower Town's market area. In the hail of paving stones, one man was killed and dozens were injured. The bloody clash became known as Stoney Monday.

Construction of the Parliament Buildings began in 1859, and by Confederation in 1867 the Centre Block was complete enough to be the seat of government of the new Dominion of Canada. But Ottawa remained little more than a lumbertown with a few official buildings until the 1890s, when Prime Minister Wilfrid Laurier began to develop plans that would help transform the dowdy city into what some referred to as "Washington of the North."

Despite Laurier's plans for a more stately capital, Ottawa continued to be defined by its shanty-town beginnings. Fire was the most effective force in reshaping the city. On a frigid night in February 1916, fire broke out inside the Centre Block of the Parliament Buildings, and within hours the building was completely gutted. Only the magnificent Parliamentary Library was saved, thanks to the efforts of a quick-thinking clerk, who closed the fireproof doors before fleeing. Reconstruction began right away, with the parliamentarians relocated for four years to the Victoria Memorial Museum Building (the site of the Canadian Museum of Nature today). Fire affected the lives of the federal politicians again in 1928, when the Russell House — a popular hotel on the city's main square, Confederation Square — burned to the ground. Another Confederation Square landmark, Ottawa's first city hall, was destroyed by fire in 1931.

The loss of the two cornerstones of the square cleared the way for construction of the distinctive National War Memorial, which was unveiled by King George VI in 1939. The War Memorial, the new Peace Tower, and the stately Château Laurier Hotel created a trademark look that could be recognized worldwide. But Confederation Square remained a gritty, grimy place. The passenger train station formed another side of it, and the smoke from the steam engines hung in the downtown air. The freight yards were situated just west of the core, creating more pollution. Rapid expansion was

Big Joe Mufferaw: lumbertown legend

Folksinger Stompin' Tom Connors popularized the story of Jos Montferrand, a francophone labourer renowned in pioneer days for his tremendous strength. Over the years, tales of his physical feats in the Ottawa Valley have turned him into a Paul Bunyan-like character called Big Joe Mufferaw. Like his American counterpart, Mufferaw is said to have created a number of features of the landscape. "Up the line" (as the Valley is often referred to) Big Joe is credited, or blamed, for any strange or unnatural occurrence.

The original Parliament Buildings, ca. 1900

threatening to run unchecked.

Enter Jacques Gréber, a French-born urban planner. In 1950, he wrote a plan for the federal government that would transform the region and give it the face it has today. His vision included a network of roads that would be incorporated into the existing parkland and a strip of green-space that would encircle

The Byward Market Square, 1922

Ottawa. It took two decades for Gréber's plan to change Ottawa, but his mark is everywhere you look in the region today. The Greenbelt continues to separate commercial areas from the suburban sprawl, and parkways prevent traffic tie-ups in the downtown core. Since 1959, the business of defining the look of the National Capital Region has been in the hands of the federally governed National Capital Commission (NCC). Today, the NCC controls 10% of all the land in the region — on both sides of the Ottawa River — and manages many aspects of the region's cultural life, including events like Winterlude, Canada Day festivities, and Cultures Canada.

The 1960s brought the sleek, octagonal National Arts Centre to Confederation Square (on the site of the old city hall), the Sparks Street Mall (the second pedestrian-only street in North America), and the transformation of the old downtown train station into a government conference centre. All train traffic was banished from the core.

Canada's centennial year, 1967, was a watershed in Ottawa's development. With the city playing host to virtually every major world leader, a number of beautification projects were completed, and others were undertaken. Aging streets were resurfaced, most of the city's electrical wiring was moved underground, and old buildings were refurbished.

Ottawa at a glance

City of Ottawa area:
110 square kilometres
(42.5 square miles)

Regional Municipality of Ottawa-Carleton area (Ottawa plus ten surrounding communities):
3185 square kilometres
(1230 square miles)

City of Ottawa population:
313,987
(12th largest in Canada)

Regional population:
900,000
(4th largest in Canada)

The face of Ottawa may have been changing, but Hull remained the same. It never shook its lumbertown roots, and in the 1960s the city was still characterized by small, wooden houses, warehouses, and working-class taverns. In 1969, the federal government announced plans to relocate several of its departments in Hull, allowing for the demolition of many of Ottawa's older buildings. The NCC led a program to redevelop Hull's core. Down came the ramshackle wooden structures. Up went glass-and-concrete office towers.

Ottawa has kept many buildings and sites of historical importance, refurbishing them with an eye towards visiting families, and the introduction of major new national cultural institutions like the Canadian Museum of Civilization, the National Gallery of Canada, the National Aviation Museum, and the Canadian Museum of Contemporary Photography has fulfilled the dream that people like Sir Wilfrid Laurier and Jacques Gréber had for Ottawa.

23

3: Getting there and getting around

Getting to Ottawa is becoming easier all the time. The number of direct flights from other cities is increasing, and a new highway leading to northern New York State and southern Ontario is under construction. And once you've arrived in the nation's capital, you'll find that getting around is not only easy but pleasant. The core area is small enough that you can walk or take a bus to most major attractions, there is an extensive network of bicycle paths, and 30 minutes' drive will take you to most of the region's outstanding sights.

Getting there

By air

Overshadowed by central Canada's commercial hubs, Ottawa has long been woefully underserviced by direct airline flights outside the Ottawa-Toronto-Montreal triangle. The situation is improving, but it still remains easier to fly here from Pittsburgh than from Winnipeg or Charlottetown. The open skies policy between Canada and the U.S. is rapidly increasing the volume of flights into Ottawa's Macdonald-Cartier International Airport.

When booking a flight, always ask about special fares; there are usually substantial reductions for flyers who stay over a specific time period or designated days of the week. If you subscribe to one of the commercial on-line services, such as

CompuServe or AOL, you can usually log on to EAASY SABRE, the database that travel agents use. This will allow you to compare flight times, fares, and other options. (EAASY SABRE will also provide a certain amount of information about accommodations, although it is by no means a complete listing.)

Children under 2 can travel free if they remain in an adult's lap, but this is not advisable for flights of over an hour's duration. If you want your child to fly seated in a car-seat, you will have to bring it yourself and pay the regular rate for a child. Airlines offer occasional discounts for children, depending on the demand for full-fare seats on the flight. Always ask about children's fare reductions. If your child is an especially picky eater or requires a special diet, be sure to ask about a special meal when you book your tickets.

Request seating directly behind the airplane's bulkhead, which will provide you with more legroom and perhaps, depending on the type of plane, a small amount of floor space for your child to play. If your child is under 6 months, request a skycot, which can be installed behind the bulkhead. If the bulkhead seats are not available when you book your flight, ask the flight attendant if it is possible to exchange seats with the passengers who hold those tickets; most people are willing to make the switch if it will make the flight more pleasant for a child.

Macdonald-Cartier International Airport

One of the airport's Kids Corners

Most airlines bend over backwards to make children's flight experiences pleasant, providing pre-boarding assistance, special magazines and games, and souvenirs of the flight. A visit to the flight deck can be the experience of a lifetime, but it is allowed only at the discretion of the pilot. Ask the flight attendant if it's possible.

Macdonald-Cartier International Airport

Ottawa's airport is small by international standards, but it has recently been renovated and is well appointed. There are no hotels in the vicinity.

On arrival — All passengers arrive on the second floor of the V-shaped terminal. Canadian Customs and Immigration and the baggage claim area are on the ground floor, as are a currency exchange service, a traveller's information booth, and car rental kiosks. Directly across the aisle from the car rental booths is a telephone hotline for making hotel reservations. Automated bank machines and a washroom with diaper-changing facilities are located in the main lobby.

On departure — The passenger check-in area is on the ground floor, at the opposite end of the terminal from the arrivals section. Located in the main lobby are a rudimentary bookstore and a gift shop with overpriced souvenirs to tempt your young ones. To reach the security area, take the main escalator directly opposite the bookstore. There are three designated Kids Corners on the second floor: one in the large area outside the security desks, and one at each end of the terminal. They are not terribly well stocked; just some Lego and an activity board. Still, they may distract young children for a short time. One advantage of the airport's compact size is that the terminal is very close to the runways, so children have plenty of opportunity to watch planes take off and land.

If you have an extended stay at the airport, there are several places to eat, ranging from a 24-hour Tim Horton's donut outlet to a full-service restaurant that is open daily 10 am–7 pm. A snackbar on the second floor is open daily 6 am–9 pm. A duty-free shop on the second floor opens one hour before international flights.

Ground transportation — The airport is south of Ottawa, about a 20-minute drive from downtown. The Airport Parkway is the main route to the city core. If you wish to rent a car during your stay, six companies operate at the airport: Avis, Budget, Dollar, Hertz, Thrifty, and Tilden.

Taxis pick up arriving passengers outside the terminal directly behind the car rental booths. The average fare to downtown is $20, plus 10¢ per bag; but the cost can be significantly higher during morning or afternoon rush hours. There is no flat-rate airport limousine service.

A hotel shuttle bus departs from the airport 6:10 am–12:20 am daily, every $1/2$ hour at 20 minutes to the hour and 10 minutes after. A one-way trip is $9 per adult, or you can pre-pay a return trip for $14. The fare for seniors and students (with ID) is $5;

Macdonald-Cartier International Airport

For information on services, call 998-1427. Call your airline for flight information. General weather information is available by calling 998-3439. A brochure outlining the airport's services can be obtained by faxing a request to 998-4379.

children under 7 ride free. On the return trip, the shuttle makes its first pick-up at Les Suites Hotel at 5 am. You don't need a hotel reservation to use the service, and the drivers will let passengers off along the route at places other than hotels.

The airport is also serviced by OC Transpo's route 96, which takes about 25 minutes to reach the downtown core using an exclusive transitway. See page 31 for fare information.

By rail

Ottawa Station is just east of Ottawa's core and is serviced by numerous VIA Rail trains that operate in the main Quebec City–Windsor rail corridor. VIA, which is Canada's national passenger rail system, competes vigorously against the airlines and intercity bus services. For both coach and first-class service (VIA 1), half-price fares are available for children 2–11; toddlers under 2 travel free on a parent's lap.

Travelling by VIA 1 is highly recommended if you will be on the train over the dinner hour, as your fare includes a very nice meal with complementary wine and digestifs. VIA 1 also guarantees reserved seating and gives you unlimited access to the first-class lounge at the train station, including free soft drinks, coffee, and juices.

Regardless of whether you travel first-class or coach, VIA provides children with cardboard train models and colouring books. Newer cars have diaper-changing tables in the washrooms.

Ottawa Station

Ottawa's train station provides only basic services, including a Burger King outlet. The VIA 1 lounge, which is reserved for first-class passengers, is far more comfortable than the rest of the terminal. On the plus side, the station has a large, open interior, giving kids a lot of room to roam. Children will also enjoy the glass-encased, large-scale model trains on display just inside the terminal's main doors.

Taxis pick up passengers at the curb outside the front doors. The average fare to downtown

Ottawa Station
General information:
244-8289

Voyageur Colonial Bus Station

is $8, plus 10¢ per bag.

The train station is a stop on one of OC Transpo's main transitways, giving you a number of options of bus routes to take downtown. See page 31 for fare information.

By bus

Intercity buses operate out of the Voyageur Colonial Bus Station on Catherine Street between Kent and Lyon Streets, about a 3-minute drive from Parliament Hill. If you are coming into Ottawa from Montreal, however, you can arrange with the driver to be let off at one of several convenient stops closer to the major hotels. Services at the bus station are very basic, including a restaurant and a small newsstand. If you find yourself there with time and children on your hands, the Canadian Museum of Nature is only a 3-block walk, and there are several neighbourhood parks nearby.

A taxi from the bus station to the major downtown hotels is about a $5 ride, plus 10¢ per bag.

OC Transpo routes 1, 4, and 7 run to/from Bank and Catherine Streets.

Voyageur Colonial Bus Station

General information:
238-5900

The Rideau Canal, with the National Arts Centre on the left

By car

Ottawa is readily accessible from all four points on the compass, although some of the highways are better routes than others. By far the best route to take into the city is Highway 417, a four-lane expressway that extends from the Quebec border in the east to about an hour outside Ottawa in the west. The road is known as the Queensway within Ottawa's borders and runs within sight of most of the city's major hotels. From Highway 401 and the U.S. border, the main connection is Highway 16, a two-lane route that terminates at Dow's Lake in the heart of the city. If you're approaching the city from the north, Quebec's Highway 5 crosses the Ottawa River on the Macdonald-Cartier Bridge and leads to several downtown city streets.

By boat

One of the most enjoyable ways to journey to Ottawa is by boat on the Rideau Canal, which runs north from Lake Ontario. The canal's exact dates of operation vary depending on the weather, but it's generally open from Victoria Day to Thanksgiving. Moorage is available in the heart of the city, adjacent to the National Arts Centre. Moorage rates are set according to the size of your boat, ranging from $6.50 per night for boats 5.5 metres (18 feet, 1 inch) and under to $19.75 per night for boats longer than 12 metres (39 feet, 4 inches). A complete list of lockage fees, schedules, and regulations is available from:

> **Superintendent,**
> **Rideau Canal**
> **34A Beckwith Street South**
> **Smiths Falls ON K7A 2A8**

Getting around town

By bus

Bus service throughout the Regional Municipality of Ottawa-Carleton and to major tourist attractions in Hull is provided by the 700 red-and-white vehicles of OC Transpo. The route system is somewhat complex, because of the irregular

Travel, the OC Transpo way

- **Fares:** To board a bus you must have either the exact change in coins (bills are discouraged because they clog the cash box) — $1.85 for riders over 11, $1 for children 6–11, children under 6 ride free — a ticket, a bus pass, or a transfer from a previous bus. Tickets can be purchased at most drugstores and convenience stores throughout the region.
- **Route information:** For information on schedules and fares, dial 741-4390, Mondays–Saturdays 6 am–11 pm; Sundays and holidays 8 am–11 pm. OC Transpo also provides an automated service that will

inform you when buses leave a specific stop. To use the service, note the four-digit number posted on the stop's sign. Dial 560 and the four digits, and a computer-generated voice will tell you when the next two buses will leave that stop. Schedule information is also displayed on electronic monitors at most major transit stops and in some shopping malls.

- **Customer service:** 748-4408, Mondays–Fridays 8:30 am–5 pm
- **Lost and found:** Located downtown at Place de Ville, Tower A; 563-4011, Mondays–Fridays 8:30 am–5 pm

31

The OC Transpo transitway

layout of Ottawa's streets. In recent years, the region has completed several sections of a transitway dedicated to buses, which allows them to bypass city streets and slower vehicles. OC Transpo provides a very detailed map of all its routes, including most tourist destinations, free of charge. You can receive it by mail by phoning 741-4390, or pick one up at the company's downtown office in Tower A of Place de Ville, Kent and Albert Streets.

While expensive by many cities' standards, OC Transpo's service is generally quite good. In fact, the system has won an award as the best transit service in North America. The drivers are usually courteous and tend to know the city fairly well.

By taxi

Ottawa's taxi drivers will get you where you're going, but don't expect much beyond perfunctory service. Taxis are not permitted to roam the streets looking for fares, although you may hail one that is not occupied. Several taxis are usually waiting to pick up passengers in front of each major hotel, or you can ask the doorman or concierge to call one. There are also two downtown taxi stands where cabbies congregate during weekdays: Metcalfe Street between Laurier Avenue and Slater Street, and Gloucester Street between Elgin and Metcalfe Streets. When returning to your hotel from another part of town, your best bet is to phone for a cab; the largest taxi company is Blue Line, 238-1111.

Taxi travel is relatively expensive in Ottawa. A cab ride from the Westin Hotel to Dow's Lake will probably cost $8, based on a fare structure of $2 plus 10¢ for each 85 metres (93 yards) or 17 seconds of standing time. There is no charge for small hand luggage such as a briefcase, but travel bags or groceries are charged at 10¢ per bag.

By car

Traffic on the Queensway and the bridges over the Ottawa River usually slows to a crawl for an hour on weekday mornings and afternoons, but at other times the city has few traffic problems. There is metered parking on most streets in the core area, and parking is usually restricted to one hour. The cost is 25¢ for 15 minutes. Be careful not to leave your car after your meter has expired or to park outside of the posted times; Ottawa's parking control officers work on commission and are not known for their flexibility.

If you are visiting between November 15 and April 1, on-street parking is prohibited overnight if more than 5 centimetres (2 inches) of snow is forecast.

There are many parking lots in downtown Ottawa, both indoor and outdoor. Those operated by the city (indicated by their signage) tend to be more expensive than the independent lots. Most lots offer early-bird discounts to people who park before 9 am. On average, the daily maximum is $8.50. The prices rise as you get closer to Parliament Hill; you can often save $2 by walking an extra few blocks.

The parking regulations in Hull are much the same as in Ottawa, with one major exception. During the summer, tourists can obtain a one-day visitors' permit that allows you to park free at meters or municipal lots. Call 819-595-7860 for more information.

4: Ottawa's Top 10 family attractions

Ottawa is Canada's national showcase. Like any capital, Ottawa is home to a number of national institutions and historic sites. Decades of tourism have honed the services of many of the city's attractions, making it difficult to choose just 10 that should not be missed. We chose the 10 attractions that follow on the basis of their unique character and their ability to draw and please visitors year after year. They are listed in alphabetical order, and those that make especially good family destinations are marked with the teddy bear stamp of approval.

1. Bicycle Paths ✱

Ottawans love their bicycles — so much so that, during the months when the ground is free of snow, about 5% of all travel in the city is done by bike. This represents about 80,000 cycling trips per day. The chronology of supply and demand is lost in the mists of recent history, but regardless of whether they met a demand or caused one, bike paths are now plentiful in the capital region.

Cycling through Major's Hill Park

At 150 kilometres (90 miles), the region's bike paths make up one of the largest such networks in North America. Bicycle-only paths crisscross the city, and many urban streets have special bike lanes. On Sundays from Victoria Day to Labour Day, 25 kilometres (15 miles) of urban parkway is closed to vehicular traffic for the benefit of bikers, walkers, joggers, and in-line skaters. It's worth noting that Ontario law requires children to wear bicycle helmets. Helmets are available if you rent bikes at Rent-a-Bike, behind the Château Laurier Hotel (see page 88); when renting from other outlets you must supply your own.

The two most popular routes for leisure bikers run west and south from the city's core. Appropriately, they cover two of the city's most scenic areas.

The **Ottawa River Parkway** runs from just west of Parliament Hill all the way to Ottawa's western border. It is flanked by a bike path that hugs the shoreline of the Ottawa (parts of the path actually flood in the early spring), and it's one of the routes that are closed to cars on Sundays. For much of its run, the parkway is built on landfill, so the terrain is relatively flat. Even the youngest tykes should have no problem. The area of the parkway just east of the

Parkdale Avenue exit offers superb views of both Ottawa and Hull.

Running south of the downtown core on both sides of the **Rideau Canal**, recreational paths provide a sidewalk-level view of some of the city's most exclusive neighbourhoods, along with a good dose of history. These paths are extremely popular with pedestrians and in-line skaters, too, so bicyclists must take care to share the road. The path on the west side of the canal offers the added advantage of running past the **Canal Ritz**, a chalet-like restaurant that juts out over the canal walls. When U.S. President Bill Clinton and his wife, Hillary, were in Ottawa in 1995, they dropped into the Canal Ritz for lunch with Prime Minister Jean Chrétien and his wife, Aline. The restaurant has a popular outdoor terrace, a great place to cool off and ease those saddle sores.

It is entirely possible to conduct your whole tour of Ottawa's sights by bike, since many of the paths and bike lanes intersect. A detailed map of the bike arteries is available from both visitor information centres (see pages 10-11).

2. Byward Market

Transit: OC Transpo routes 2, 3, 4, 6, 7, 14, and 18 pass by or through the Market

By strict definition, the Byward Market is a one-block indoor/outdoor produce and craft market consisting of a central building and a number of individual stores, five minutes' walk from Parliament Hill. In broader terms, though, the Market is a commercial area that stretches four blocks from Sussex Drive in the west to King Edward Avenue in the east, and six blocks from St. Patrick Street in the north to Besserer Street in the south. This was the business sector of Bytown's Lower Town, and some of the stone buildings from that era are still in use. The Market was the site of the infamous Stoney Monday Riot in 1849 (see page 19), and it was where farmers from miles around brought their goods for sale in the last century. The current produce market dates back to 1927, but the rejuvenation of the Market into the place where urban Ottawa comes to eat, drink, and shop

The Byward Market on a busy Saturday

has been under way for less than 20 years.

The Market fell out of favour with proper Ottawans during the early part of the 20th century when, with its mix of taverns, discount stores, and greasy-spoon restaurants, it certainly wasn't the kind of place for parents to take their kids. By the 1960s, the Market was as close to a red-light district as conservative Ottawa ever came. The turnaround began with the birth of the Market's first trendy, upscale restaurants in the late 1970s. Slowly, almost imperceptibly, over the next decade, the neighbourhood changed, with boutiques replacing century-old drygoods stores and large, bright restaurants replacing the old grills. The pace of change picked up in the late 1980s, and today the Market is almost unrecognizable to long-time Ottawans.

Each day begins early on the Market, as farmers transfer their produce from truck beds to sidewalk stalls. The activity runs year-round, with maple syrup, Christmas trees, and firewood replacing the fresh produce as winter sets in. Throughout the year, the streets surrounding the central Market building, off George Street, buzz from just after sunrise, as chefs from the city's best restaurants scour the stalls and indoor stores for the ingredients of that day's meals.

37

By 7:30 am on weekdays, the neighbourhood's breakfast spots have filled up with businesspeople stopping off for a bagel and a coffee on the way to their uptown offices. From the first warm spring day until the air takes on the fall chill in October, sidewalk cafés rule the Market, and throughout the summer the neighbourhood is chock-a-block with patio umbrellas. The action doesn't slow down until 1 am, with university-aged young people crowding the sidewalks as they move between dance clubs, restaurants, and live-music establishments.

But the Market isn't only for habitués of upscale bars and restaurants. Given its diversity of shops and food outlets, the Market offers something for almost any taste and any budget. The neighbourhood's close proximity to many of the city's major tourist attractions also makes it an ideal "junction" for your day. You can hit the Market early in the morning to choose the ingredients for a picnic lunch, or to pick up some delicious ready-made sandwiches from **Fraser's Food Shop** at 117-C Parent Street. After a few hours at the National Gallery of Canada or a visit to Laurier House (see pages 75-77), chill your kids out with the fabulous gelato at **Piccolo Grande**, 55 Murray Street. Or when your preteens have grown weary of hearing about history, lead them to the **Sassy Bead Company** at 11 William Street, where they can spend up to an hour or two picking out the components of awesome earrings or chokers from the huge selection of beads and baubles. The store even has a worktable where they can string together their new fashion statements. (For more Byward Market shops, see pages 92-93.)

In short, there's little that can't be found in some corner of the Market, and most trips to Ottawa will involve skirting it or strolling through it to reach a destination.

3. Canadian Museum of Civilization ✱

Where? 100 Laurier Street, Hull
819-776-7000
Internet: http://www.cmcc.muse.digital.ca/cmchome.html

The dramatic exterior of the Museum of Civilization

Transit: OC Transpo route 8 to Laurier and Papineau Streets

When? May 1 to June 30, Labour Day to Thanksgiving, daily 9 am–6 pm, Thursdays 9 am–9 pm; Canada Day to Labour Day, Saturdays–Wednesdays 9 am–6 pm, Thursdays and Fridays 9 am–9 pm; Thanksgiving to April 30, Tuesdays–Sundays 9 am–5 pm, Thursdays 9 am–9 pm, closed Mondays. The Children's Museum: May 1 to Thanksgiving, 9 am–6 pm; Thanksgiving to April 30, 9 am–5 pm, closed Mondays.

How much? $12 for families, $5 for adults, $3.50 for seniors and youths (13–18), $1 for children 2–12, children under 2 free; admission free Sundays 9 am–noon; admission to the CINÉPLUS is extra

How long? No less than 4 hours

Extras: First-class restaurant, cafeteria, snackbar, exceptional gift shop, children's boutique, fully wheelchair and stroller accessible, strollers and wheelchairs available free from the cloakroom, diaper-changing facilities in all washrooms, parking $8 per day, locker rental $1

Even without exhibits, the Canadian Museum of Civilization would be on a shortlist of must-see attractions in the capital region. Designed by native Canadian architect Douglas Cardinal and completed in 1989, it is a stunning-looking building with panoramic views of downtown Ottawa. But the museum *does* have exhibits, put together from some 3.75 million collected artifacts and displayed in 16,500 square metres (178,000 square feet) over three floors. Its exhibits cover the entire scope of human life, with emphasis on the Canadian perspective. Among the highlights are impressive West Coast Indian totem poles and live re-creations of historical events. Stop at the information desk just inside the front doors and pick up a copy of "Today's Events" to find out about special craft and interpretive programs.

Some galleries are still under development, but there is enough to keep your family entertained for hours. In an age when museums rely increasingly on high-tech displays to tell a story, the Museum of Civilization engages visitors the old-fashioned way: by firing up their imaginations. Our kids haven't tired of the place yet, even after dozens of visits.

The entrance to the **Children's Museum** — across the lobby from the ticket counter — is so innocuous that it gives no indication of the fun that lies within. Forget appearances, though; the Children's Museum has become the soul of the Museum of Civilization. Children must be 14 or under to enter, and those under 10 must be accompanied by an adult. Any group of five children must be accompanied by at least one adult. Those are about the only restrictions imposed here; the emphasis is on hands-on play, and there is no shortage of material to help kids learn through doing. Kids love climbing aboard the garish Pakistani bus, dressing up in period costumes, and getting their "passports" stamped at various points throughout the museum. The Children's Museum has an overarching international theme, and the hub of any visit is the **Embassy**. There you can register for a workshop or find out more about a specific exhibit. The staff is young, bright, and very helpful.

Throughout the year, the museum stages about 1500 workshops and special events, often with themes to match a season or ethnic holiday. These fall under a few broad categories: Shared Time, a program for children under 5 and their parents; Kids in the Kitchen; Family Programs, where children learn about Hallowe'en traditions, how to make a kite, or how Swedes celebrate Christmas; and Youthworks!, an in-depth series aimed at kids 10 to 14 that allows them to work on a project with experts in specialized fields. Preregistration in person is required on the day of the workshop.

In addition to the workshops and special events, the Children's Museum has a major exhibit space called **Kaleidoscope**, which features displays from the Museum of Civilization and other children's museums from around the world. Upcoming exhibits include "The Magic School Bus — Inside the Earth" (October 31, 1996, to February 2, 1997) and a Winter Fun Poster Challenge (February 1997).

Even the most dedicated parent can get a bit overwhelmed after an hour or so in the Children's Museum, where the noise level tends to hover around that of a very unruly school assembly. If you long for a break from a school-aged child, book him or her into the secure crafts room and head through the Children's Boutique towards the back of the museum building. Just outside the boutique on the right you'll find the Lunch Box, a small take-out snackbar, where you can order cappuccino or other refreshments. On one side of the large open area — which is where group tours are met by museum guides — are some comfortable leather chairs and couches where you can enjoy your break in blissful peace.

If you have kids young enough for admittance to the Children's Museum, you'll probably want more than a coffee break before taking

West Coast Indian totem poles at the Museum of Civilization

them to see more of the main exhibits. The museum houses a number of options for lunch, and the Hull neighbourhood outside the museum has little to offer. In addition to the main restaurant, which is relatively pricey, there is a better-than-average cafeteria, as well as the Lunch Box. If the weather's nice, the grounds offer ample opportunity for children to run off some energy. And in any weather, the views of Ottawa from this vantage point will generate contemplative thoughts of Champlain, By, and Macdonald, and what the area must have looked like in their eras.

Second to the Children's Museum, the area that thrills kids the most is the one on the lower level that's devoted to telling the story of Canada's First Peoples. The re-creation of a **West Coast native building** catches the eye from the tall escalator that transports you from the main floor. The large area at the front of this tableau is often used for concerts as part of the Cultures Canada festival (see pages 134-35) and gives the museum a tremendous sense of space.

Behind the façade are numerous displays depicting the lives of various aboriginal nations.

Canada's other founding cultures are represented on the third floor, where the **Canada Hall**'s displays trace the country's history from the arrival of Norse explorers up to a re-creation of a 19th-century village. As you look at the exhibits, you might find yourself swept up in the action of a play, whose characters seem to step out of the displays around you. The actors are adept at tailoring their lines and actions to suit the size of the audience.

A mezzanine floor and additional space on the main level are used for temporary exhibits. Running throughout 1996 are exhibits of Québécois folk art and a look at the evolution of hats that kids will probably enjoy as much as adults. Also on the main floor is the **CINÉPLUS theatre**, which shows IMAX and OMNIMAX films at scheduled times throughout the day. The films vary from studies of Yellowstone National Park to concert footage of the Rolling Stones and can be seen

for an additional charge, usually in the $5–$8 range. The CINÉPLUS was the first theatre in the world to use the Canadian-made big-screen technology, and it remains one of the few OMNIMAX cinemas in North America. If a film is new or extremely popular, tickets can be hard to come by. It's advisable to phone ahead for reservations and avoid disappointment.

4. Canadian Museum of Nature ✱

Where? At Metcalfe and McLeod Streets
996-3102
Transit: OC Transpo route 6 to Elgin and McLeod Streets
When? May 1 to Labour Day, daily 9:30 am–5 pm, Thursdays 9:30 am–8 pm; Labour Day to April 30, daily 10 am–5 pm, Thursdays 10 am–8 pm
How much? $9 for families, $4 for adults, $3 for students over 16, $2 for seniors and children 6–16, children under 6 free; admission half-price Thursdays until 5 pm, free

The castle-like exterior of the Museum of Nature

Thursdays after 5 pm and Canada Day

How long? No less than 3 hours

Extras: Cafeteria, gift shop with large selection of nature books, mineral boutique, partially wheelchair and stroller accessible, strollers available free at the cloakroom, diaper-changing tables in washrooms on first and third floors, parking $7 per day

Everybody loves castles, so the Canadian Museum of Nature, located a leisurely 15-minute walk from Parliament Hill, naturally attracts kids as soon as they spot its turrets, buttresses, and parapets. David Ewart's 1910 Victoria Memorial Museum Building has been described by various puzzled observers as "free Gothic," "Tudor Gothic," and "Scottish baronial." The building's atrium, stained-glass windows, and grand staircases are striking.

One of the real strengths of the Museum of Nature is its **children's animation area**, behind the gift boutique on the first floor, where cheerful docents help kids learn through various projects, puppet shows, and games. The theme of this area for the next five years will be the medicinal uses of plants.

Rockhounds will love the **Viola MacMillan Mineral Gallery** on the second floor, which has some eye-catching displays of gold and other precious metals and stones. Included is a retail outlet where collectors can add to their treasures.

The mineral gallery leads to a major highlight of the building: a mock-up of the **Abitibi gold mine** in northern Ontario. A left turn at the entrance to the display brings you abruptly to the staging area of the mine itself. As you wait for the door of the mine elevator to open, you can watch a video of a miner describing what it's like to work underground or examine the miners' gear that is mounted on the walls. A dozen ominous miners' suits hang over your head like stalactites. Then a red light begins to flash and the door to the elevator rolls up. If anyone in your family has traces of claustrophobia, they'll probably show up at this point. The elevator is appropriately dark and dank, and the simulated descent into the mine is real enough to frighten younger children. When the door on the other side of the car opens, you walk out into a realistic mineshaft, where kids can get behind a pneumatic drill or examine what gold deposits look like when they're still embedded in the rock. The safety mesh covering the overhead rock and the timbers that have been wedged into the walls are suitably creepy. How realistic is the mine? Realistic enough that museum officials have to stop some overenthusiastic kids from bringing hammers with them to chip samples off the walls.

The **Time Machine** is another virtual-reality display, albeit one with more of a fantasy bent than the mine. The flashing lights and sound effects won't fool even the youngest visitors, but the recorded script is amusing and clever. Fifteen minutes in the Time Machine will teach children more about the origins of the Earth than an hour spent staring at the museum's ordinary displays in the Earth section on the first floor.

Creepy Critters on the third floor brings visitors face to face with some animals and insects that humans usually try to avoid. Eels, leeches, slugs, beetles, and rats may not be the most attractive creatures,

Inside the Museum of Nature's gold mine

but kids are fascinated by them. Kids love dinosaurs, too, of course, and the **dino exhibit** at the museum has been a mainstay for more than 80 years. In 1913, the museum made its name in the scientific community when its paleontologists discovered the 70-million-year-old bones of *Edmontosaurus*, one of the largest and best-preserved dinosaurs to be found. Adults may appreciate the significance of *Edmontosaurus*, which is the main attraction in the dino room, but children who have seen the dinosaurs at larger museums in Toronto or New York City will be disappointed at the small collection here.

Another niggling let-down at the Museum of Nature is that many of the exhibits are of the static variety, including quite a few dioramas of birds and mammals, and some of the displays are showing their age. It's not unusual to find exhibit captions that have been worn off, or display case glass that has cracked. Even given those reservations, there is plenty here to keep children, especially younger ones, enthralled for several hours.

5. Central Experimental Farm

Where? Experimental Farm Drive (formerly National Capital Commission Driveway) at Prince of Wales Drive 991-3044

Transit: OC Transpo route 3 to Prince of Wales Drive and Experimental Farm Drive

When? Grounds: year-round daily sunrise to sunset; Agriculture Museum: March to November 9 am–5 pm, closed December to February; animal barns: March to October 9 am–5 pm, November to February 10 am–4 pm

How much? Museum and barns: $7 for families, $3 for adults, $2 for seniors, youths (17 and 18), and children 3–16, children under 3 free; grounds and arboretum free

How long? 3 hours

Extras: Gift shop, fully wheelchair and stroller accessible, diaper-change facilities, parking is free

This 500-hectare (1236-acre) Agriculture Canada property gives Ottawa the unique feature of having a working farm within a 10-minute drive of its urban core. Created in 1886 as one of five research farms across the country, the Central Experimental Farm continues to operate primarily as a scientific facility, but several parts in the northeast sector are open to the public. Everything is within easy walking distance, and the relaxed pace of life on the farm can provide a welcome break from a round of urban sightseeing. Pack a picnic lunch in the summer, or bring along a toboggan for some winter action on the adjacent hills. You can pay admission to tour the exhibits and animal barns, or simply wander freely among the ornamental gardens and trees.

If farming is in your family's background, the museum may not hold anything novel for your children, but urban kids are intrigued by how food was produced in the 1920s. In addition to the antique farm implements, the **Agriculture Museum** features a long-running exhibit called **The Amazing Potato**. Like the farm

In the cattle barn at the Experimental Farm

itself, the display lacks the whiz-bang interactivity of some of Ottawa's other museums, but it manages to make effective use of the humble tuber to trace the social and economic development of the country. The museum's gift shop is also relatively low-key, and usually has a stock of quality barnyard animal toys at reasonable prices.

Urban or rural, few kids can withstand the lure of baby animals, and there's no shortage of them down on the farm, especially in the late winter and spring. There are five separate **animal barns**, one each for dairy and beef cattle, pigs, sheep, and horses. Since this *is* an experimental farm, it has a higher-than-average variety of breeds, including some types of dairy cattle and swine that are rarely seen elsewhere in Canada. Regardless of what time of year you visit, children will discover the animals at some interesting stage in their development, although spring is always special with so many newborns around. The warming pens in the swine barn are a favourite area where children can peer through large windows to watch the baby pigs as they lie pressed together with their siblings. In another section, older pigs vie for their mother's attention and an extra helping of milk. For sheer size at the other end of the growth scale, nothing can match the magnificent Clydesdale horses.

During March Break, the farm offers special children's activities, including feeding and milking cows, grinding grain, making bread, and various farm crafts. In early August, during Field Days, children have an opportunity to see crops growing and watch them being processed into pasta, flour, and beer. During October, kids can participate in sheep-shearing, see grain being threshed, and watch fruit being preserved.

East of the museum and animal barns, and running from the traffic circle on Prince of Wales Drive down a terraced hill to the Rideau Canal, is the **Dominion Arboretum and Botanic Garden**, an integral part of the farm. Ostensibly a display of exotic trees from around the world, the arboretum is also a first-rate urban oasis, on a par with Montreal's Mount Royal or Vancouver's Stanley Park. You enter the arboretum on a narrow road that branches off the traffic circle connecting Prince of Wales and Experimental Farm Drive. The road circles a lovely thicket of pine trees and is bordered on the opposite side by a thick stone wall that children can't resist climbing. The wall provides a fine view of downtown Ottawa, Dow's Lake, and Carleton University. From your perch on the wall you can also determine your best route to the bottom of the arboretum's hill, which, depending on your sense of adventure and your fitness level, might be one of the gentle bicycle paths that traverse the hill or straight down across the grass (the preferred route of younger children).

In addition to the fine selection of trees, the lower section of the arboretum provides many picturesque picnic sites on the banks of the Rideau. If you don't fancy climbing back up the hill, you can carry on to the south end of the arboretum, cross the canal using the footbridges at Hartwells Locks, and catch a bus on the Carleton University campus to take you back downtown.

6. National Aviation Museum

Where? Aviation Parkway at Rockcliffe Airport 993-2010 or 1-800-463-2038
Transit: OC Transpo route 95 to Blair Road Transit

Station, transfer to route 198 to end of its route

When? May 1 to Labour Day, daily 9 am–5 pm, Thursdays 9 am–9 pm; Labour Day to April 30, Tuesdays–Sundays 9 am–5 pm, Thursdays 9 am–9 pm, holiday Mondays 9 am–5 pm, closed other Mondays

How much? $10 for families, $5 for adults, $4 for seniors and students, $1.75 for children 6–15, free for children under 6; free admission Thursdays after 5 pm

How long? No less than 2 hours

Extras: Cafeteria, fully wheelchair and stroller accessible, strollers free at cloakroom, diaper-change facilities, parking is free, audio guide $2, 15-minute biplane tour of the city $46.73, 30-minute tour of the Gatineau Hills $95

Located at the far eastern edge of Ottawa, at the Rockcliffe Airport, the National Aviation Museum is a little off the beaten track for tourists, but it's worth the extra time if there's an aviation buff in your family. If you don't have your own transportation, you can reach the museum by OC Transpo. It's much easier, however, to make the museum a stop on one of the bus tours that leave from Confederation Square (see pages 89-91).

Built in 1988, the triangular museum is stuffed with 118 vintage aircraft, representing Canada's colourful history in the air. Included is a reproduction of the **Silver Dart**, the plane that telephone pioneer Alexander Graham Bell helped to design. Taking off from the frozen surface of Baddeck Bay in Nova Scotia in February 1909, the *Silver Dart* completed the first successful manned flight in the British Empire. There are also examples of the rickety biplanes that Canadian aces like Billy Bishop flew in World War I, float-planes that helped Canadians explore the Far North, a Spitfire from World War II, and all that remains from the ill-fated project to build a world-class fighter jet, the Avro Arrow, in the 1950s.

In addition to the aircraft, the museum has a number of educational displays, including a scale-model wind tunnel that demonstrates the princi-

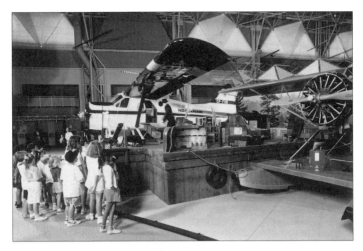

A bush plane at the Aviation Museum

ples that keep airplanes aloft. Already a state-of-the-art museum when it was built, the Aviation Museum has benefitted more recently from a pilot project in digital imaging and advanced fibre optics technology run by Kodak and Canada's telephone companies. At several places in the museum, visitors can sit at terminals and call up archival film of some of the planes in flight or additional information about their history. If you have a computer whiz with you, you'll have a hard time tearing him or her away. The museum won't hold the interest of younger children for long, though, since most of the aircraft displays are strictly "look but don't touch."

There's a cafeteria on the catwalk that runs around the perimeter of the building, but the museum's park-like setting makes it an ideal place to eat a picnic lunch.

If you have an adventurous child who's fascinated with vintage planes, you can pre-book a tour of either Ottawa or the Gatineau Hills in an open-cockpit biplane, from Victoria Day to Thanksgiving. The child must be at least 45 kilograms (100 pounds) and not afraid of steep ascents and descents. Only one person at a time can fly with the pilot. Needless to say, the plane operates only in good weather.

The National Gallery of Canada

7. National Gallery of Canada

Where? 380 Sussex Drive 990-1985
Internet: http://www.chin. gc.ca/CHIN/CHINIndex/ Homepage/ngc/en_ngc.html
Transit: OC Transpo route 3 to Sussex Drive and St. Patrick Street
When? Daily 10 am–6 pm, Thursdays 10 am–8 pm
How much? Free admission to the permanent collection; for special exhibits, adult and seniors fees vary but children under 18 and full-time students are admitted free
How long? No less than 3 hours
Extras: Cafeteria, several fine restaurants, terrific bookstore and gift shop, fully wheelchair and stroller accessible, strollers available free at Group Tour Desk, diaper-change tables in all washrooms, parking $8.50 daily maximum, audio guides

Like the Canadian Museum of Civilization, the National Gallery of Canada's new building is a showcase for one of the country's finest architects. Moshe Safdie's glass masterpiece subtly parallels the design of the Parliament Buildings and the Château Laurier Hotel and floods the

Abstract Expressionism at the National Gallery

major exhibition spaces with light. Aside from adding a breathtaking jewel to the Ottawa skyline, Safdie's design allows the art to breathe, which promotes discussion and debate. As well as the art is displayed, there is no sense of cloying pretension. Kids enjoy the fact that the art can be enjoyed without having to work at it.

Opened in 1988, with space for 1900 works, the building has allowed the National Gallery to display substantial parts of its permanent collection. This includes a large number of works by Canadians like the Group of Seven and Emily Carr, and international artists throughout the ages. Of the European masters, the gallery has a number of fine works by Cézanne, Degas, and Monet. One strength of the collection is the representation of contemporary artists like Jackson Pollock, Andy Warhol, and Barnett Newman.

The gallery's purchase of Newman's *Voice of Fire* — three broad stripes of colour — stirred a national controversy a few years ago, and the **Abstract Expressionism room** where it is displayed never fails to create familial debates. Kids invariably claim that they could paint something as good, and parents — regardless of how they feel about Expressionism — wind up defending art for art's sake. To learn more about Expressionism, pick one of the four comfortable chairs and scan the easy-to-understand brochures that explain the features of each of the pieces.

The art isn't confined to painting, either. The lower level holds a large display of **Inuit prints and sculpture**, which always seem to capture the imagination of younger children. Like the sculptors, kids under 10 seem to have the ability to sense the soul of a piece of stone.

Another highlight of the gallery is the reconstructed 19th-century **Convent of Our Lady of the Sacred Heart chapel**, which was originally situated on Ottawa's Rideau Street. Its neo-Gothic vaulted ceiling is a prime example of religious decorative art in Canada; younger kids will be fascinated just to find a complete building inside the confines of a larger one.

If, like us, you have a budding artist in your family, you'll be hard pressed to leave the gallery without an extended visit to the Bookstore on the main floor. Fortunately, items are available in a wide range of prices, and with a little coaxing you can convince your young shopper to substitute a few postcards for that expensive art book.

The gallery is near a large number of restaurants on the western edge of the Byward Market, but its Cafétéria des Beaux-Arts, which is open daily until 4 pm, competes nicely on the basis of price and atmosphere. It would be difficult to find more attractive lunchtime surroundings in a cafeteria setting.

8. National Museum of Science and Technology ✱

Where? 1867 St. Laurent Boulevard
991-3044
Transit: OC Transpo route 85 to St. Laurent Boulevard and Smyth Road
When? May 1 to Canada Day, daily 9 am–6 pm, Thursdays 9 am–9 pm; Canada Day to Labour Day, daily 9 am–6 pm, Thursdays and Fridays 9 am–9 pm; Labour Day to April 30, Tuesdays–Sundays 9 am–

The Crazy Kitchen at the Museum of Science and Technology

5 pm, closed Mondays and Christmas Day
How much? $12 for families, $6 for adults, $5 for seniors and students, $2 for children 6–15, children under 6 free
How long? No less than 4 hours
Extras: Cafeteria, fully wheelchair and stroller accessible, strollers available free, plenty of free parking, lockers 25¢, children's birthday parties can be arranged

Even after more than 25 years, the Museum of Science and Technology remains a favourite of school tours and adults who want to know how things work. The museum attracts more than 400,000 visitors a year. In fact, the museum may house the single most popular destination for kids in Ottawa: the **Crazy Kitchen**. The exhibit, which invites visitors to try to walk normally through a kitchen that has been tilted several degrees, has been there since the museum's earliest years, and it still packs them in.

The other long-time favourite display is equally user-friendly: locomotives. Housed in a huge anteroom to the main museum, the gleaming **steam engines** entice the nose first. There is something about the smell of grease — the thick, black kind that lubricated the massive driving

55

wheels and couplings of steam locomotives — that speaks of bygone days. The very size of the engines is also a draw. Small children could be frightened by machinery that's this tall, but when they can mount wooden stairs, sit in the engineer's seat, and lean an elbow out the window, intimidation turns into mastery. Adults old enough to have lived in the Age of Steam will also be intrigued by the dials, levers, and spigots that confronted engineers and firemen.

For children who live more in the present, the contemporary equivalent of riding the rails is to be Roberta Bondar or Chris Hadfield, and the museum has no shortage of **space-age gear**. Kids are more likely to be attracted by the prospect of standing inside a replica of the bay that houses the Canadarm, while you may find the details of Canada's early achievements in space equally interesting. The mockup of the 1960s-vintage NASA capsule will make you shudder at the thought of hurtling into Earth orbit packed shoulder to shoulder like so many astronaut sardines. And for those who have wondered how you shower or sleep in space, there are contraptions to show how it's done.

Connexions, a major exhibit of Canada's role in the development of telecommunications technology, brings visitors back to Earth. Most kids know that telephone inventor Alexander Graham Bell was a Canadian; lesser known are the country's achievements in digital communications, radio, TV, and fibre optics. In addition to artifacts from the early decades of telecommunications, Connexions provides hands-on displays of how we'll communicate in the future.

Demonstrating static electricity at the Museum of Science and Technology

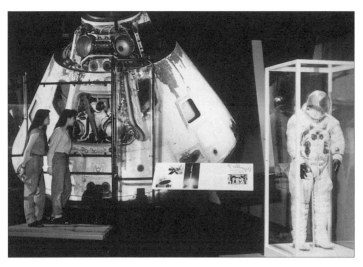

The NASA capsule at the Museum of Science and Technology

Related to Connexions is **Beyond the Printed Word**, the museum's extensive collection of vintage radios and TVs, as well as some landmark broadcasts from both media. The broadcasts are arranged by decade, so you can tune in Canadian war correspondent Matthew Halton reporting on World War II, revisit CBS news anchor Walter Cronkite announcing the death of John F. Kennedy, or watch Paul Henderson's goal from the 1972 Canada–U.S.S.R. hockey tournament. Kids get a kick out of the vintage living rooms, the same rooms that give adults a twinge of nostalgia.

In **Technology Park**, on the museum's grounds, you can examine a Saskatchewan pump jack, an Atlas rocket, a lighthouse from Cape North, Nova Scotia, a 1920s-vintage windmill, and a rebuilt Canadian Pacific Railway station.

In addition to the ongoing exhibits, the museum has a number of special programs worth asking about. The museum is home to Canada's largest refracting telescope and frequently holds astronomy evenings that include films, lectures, and first-hand observation. Call 991-9219 for schedules and registration information. Half-day science workshops are held on weekends for children 9–12;

57

call 990-7401 for times, topics, and fees. During Christmas holidays and March Break, seasonal activities and demonstrations are staged; call 990-7401.

9. Parliament Hill ✱

Where? Wellington Street between Elgin and Bank Streets
Changing the Guard: 993-1811
Centre Block Tours: 239-5000
Internet: http://www.parl. gc.ca/PIO/english/intro.html
Transit: OC Transpo routes 2, 7, 14, and 18 go past the Hill
When? Parliament Hill is open daily from 9 am throughout the year; closing times can vary during special events, such as visits by foreign heads of state, but are generally 8 pm weekdays and 5 pm weekends and statutory holidays
How much? Free
How long? No less than 2 hours
Extras: Snackbar, fully wheelchair and stroller accessible, diaper-changing facilities in outdoor public washrooms only, no public parking; 45-minute tours are available every 30 minutes daily except Christmas Day, New Year's Day, and Canada Day

As both the seat of Canadian government and a prime example of Gothic architecture, the Parliament Buildings remain the premier attraction for tourists of all ages and origins as well as Ottawa's central landmark. But there is more to Parliament Hill than politicians and beautiful stonework; the place teems with history.

There is no public parking on the Hill, and vehicular traffic is limited to the ubiquitous green mini-buses that ferry members of Parliament, senators, and their aides to and fro. Visitors can park free for one hour at the World Exchange Plaza three blocks south (enter from Metcalfe Street at Albert Street). Take your parking stub to the Canada's Capital Information Centre at 14 Metcalfe Street for validation.

The best way to enter the grounds on foot is through the large stone-and-iron gates on

The Centre Block on Parliament Hill

Wellington Street at the north end of Metcalfe Street. From this location you can appreciate the beauty of the site and the graceful proportions of the three component buildings: the **Centre Block**, which incorporates the Peace Tower, both houses of Parliament, and the Parliamentary Library; and the **East** and **West Blocks**, which house parliamentarians and are closed to the public.

Immediately inside the main gates is a statue of **Sir Galahad**, erected by future prime minister William Lyon Mackenzie King in honour of his close friend Henry Harper. Harper, a 29-year-old senior bureaucrat, drowned in 1901 while attempting to save two friends who had broken through the Ottawa River ice during a skating party. Further up the paved walkway towards the Centre Block is the **Centennial Flame**, a low natural-gas fountain that was ignited on New Year's Eve, 1966, to celebrate Canada's 100th birthday. It was planned that the flame would be extinguished at the end of 1967, but it proved so popular that the government reversed its decision and kept it burning.

On mornings between mid-May and late August, you'll want to time your visit to the Hill to correspond with the **Changing the Guard** ceremony, which takes place daily on the lawn in front of the Peace

The Changing the Guard ceremony on Parliament Hill

Tower (weather permitting) at 10 am. With its roots in British military tradition, the ceremony is a colourful display by the Governor General's Foot Guards, who wear red plumes in their tall black bearskin busbies, and the Canadian Grenadier Guards, who wear white plumes.

During the summer, stop at the large white tent between the Centre Block and West Block. It's open from Victoria Day to Labour Day from 9 am daily (except Canada Day). Here you can book indoor tours or pick up a booklet that will help you conduct your own self-paced tour of the grounds. National Capital Commission staff are on hand to help you understand what's available, and younger children will enjoy meeting Peace Tower Pete, a puppet who helps out. If you have 10-to-15-year-olds in tow and need a break from each other, guided youth tours are available by reservation (call 239-5100). The information tent also makes an ideal rendezvous spot, since public washrooms and an outdoor snackbar are located nearby.

Easily spotted on the Hill and always a hit with visitors

The Parliamentary Library

of all ages are the officers of the Royal Canadian Mounted Police. The Mounties who are chosen for ceremonial Hill duty qualify by their ability to be first-rate tourist ambassadors. Although they are not generally on horseback on the Hill, they dress in the traditional scarlet tunics and dark blue riding breeches that made the force famous. They are more than willing to pose for photos.

The televising of Parliamentary proceedings in recent years has removed some of the mystery of what goes on inside the Centre Block, but the halls where Canada's laws are made still hold a certain fascination. The **Centre Block tour** includes a quick peek at both the Red Chamber (the **Senate**) and the Green Chamber (the **House of Commons**) when the legislators are not in session. But for most people the highlight of the tour is the glimpse it gives you of the huge **Parliamentary Library**. Completed in 1876, the circular room is dominated by a towering marble figure of Queen Victoria and crowned by magnificent carved wooden bookcases.

The tour also visits the **Peace Tower**, with its 53-bell

carillon and an **observation deck** 92 metres (303 feet) up. (The carillon and deck are scheduled to reopen in mid-1996, although other renovations to the building complex will continue for some time.)

In the tower's chapel-like **Memorial Chamber**, the pages in the Books of Remembrance are turned each day at 11 am, revealing dozens of names of the men and women who died fighting in Canada's wars.

Any political junkies in your family may want a closer look at our lawmakers in action than the tour provides, which is possible when Parliament is sitting. Visitors can attend Question Period in the public galleries of either the House of Commons (call 992-4793 for times) or the Senate (992-4791). Young children will be bored to squirming by the proceedings, but anyone who's studied Parliament could find them addictive.

Be sure to take a walk around the back of the Hill to see the many statues of influential Canadians, along with a bell from the original Centre Block, the only artifact that remains from the frigid night of February 3, 1916, when every-thing but the Parliamentary Library was reduced to ashes in a massive fire. Legend has it that the bell crashed through the flames to the ground after tolling midnight on the fateful night. The view from the cliff at the rear of the Centre Block also provides an interesting perspective on the Quebec side of the Ottawa River. If you're heading to Lower Town from here, you could take the stairs that are cut into the cliff's face; they lead to a path that follows the river back to the locks at the mouth of the Rideau Canal. The steps are steep, but benches provide rest spots for the leg-weary.

Another view of history is played out on the face of the Parliament Buildings themselves as part of "Reflections of Canada: A Symphony of Sound and Light," which is performed twice nightly during the summer, except when Parliament is sitting or the weather is bad. There is seating for 700 in bleachers, and the shows alternate between English and French performances. Check at the white information tent for show times, or call 239-5100.

10. Rideau Canal ✱

What began as a strategic afterthought to the War of 1812 and turned into a classic case of man against nature has ended up defining the city of Ottawa. The Rideau Canal stretches 202 kilometres (126 miles) from the Ottawa River to Lake Ontario at Kingston, but it is the 8-kilometre (5-mile) stretch of the waterway between Hog's Back, near the campus of Carleton University, and Sapper's Bridge, at Confederation Square, that draws the most attention (and the only year-round traffic).

There is something about the well-defined stone walls of the canal and the lush vegetation that grows along most of its run through the city that symbolizes Ottawa. This is a well-cared-for place, the canal seems to say; it has its own leisurely pace. It is difficult to sightsee in Ottawa without the canal as a backdrop, and it is impossible to imagine what the city would have become had the canal not been built.

The inextricable link between the city and the canal dates back to both their origins. What they share is the legacy of John By, a lieutenant-colonel in the British Corps of

Dow's Lake Pavilion

Royal Engineers. In 1826, By was a rugged career soldier of 47, appointed to build the waterway as an alternative supply line to the garrison at Kingston should hostilities with the United States flare up again. The plans had been drawn up by a man named Samuel Clowes. By quickly discovered that Clowes knew a lot about engineering but little about geography. Clowes's plan called for the canal to be built through several swamps, including one large bog where Dow's Lake is today. In the summer of 1828, a year after the first stone was laid by Arctic explorer Sir John Franklin, 400 of By's men were struck down by malaria. Those who survived worked for another three summers to complete what was one of the greatest engineering feats of the 19th century.

The canal project shaped not only Bytown itself (By laid out the original town plan as part of his duties) but also many of the bedroom communities that lie to the south of the capital today. In return for their work on the canal, By's senior officers were given parcels of land along the Rideau, and their names live on in towns and villages from Ottawa to Kingston.

Two of the best places to see the canal are at either end of the Ottawa stretch. From Dow's Lake, the two **Hartwells Locks** and the two **Hog's Back** locks allow boats to climb gradually to the top of the sharp ridge where the canal meets the Rideau River. On the other side of the "hog's back" is a rough, rocky waterfall. The falls at Hog's Back (also called Prince of Wales Falls) is a favourite spot for photographers, especially in the spring when the runoff from the upper Rideau River swells it to a raging torrent. The trees at the adjacent Dominion Arboretum and Vincent Massey Park also make it an exceptionally pretty setting when the fall foliage is at its blazing peak. The view from the top of the falls is impressive, but if your children are beyond the stroller stage, you can follow the path down from the parking lot east of the falls and find a peaceful refuge on the large rocks where the overflow of rushing water eddies, with a better perspective on the cascade above.

The Ottawa Locks

The dominant feature of the northern end of the canal is the series of eight locks that allow boats to climb up the steep cliff from the Ottawa River like so many salmon on their way to spawn. You can see the **Ottawa Locks** from below on an Ottawa Riverboat Company tour (see page 88), or look down over them from Sapper's Bridge, at Confederation Square. Either perspective will give kids an understanding of how astonishingly difficult it was to build the canal and its locks with the tools of the 1820s.

There are paths and staircases going down from Sapper's Bridge and along both sides of the upper locks, and footbridges crossing over them. (For a stroller-accessible route to the locks, head for Major's Hill Park on the north side of the Château Laurier Hotel.) From here you can see the machinery up close and watch boats being lifted in the warm-weather months. It can take as long as $2\frac{1}{2}$ hours for a boat to climb all eight locks, ending up 24 metres (79 feet) above the river.

Of course, the best way to appreciate the canal is by using it. If you didn't arrive in the capital by boat, you can get a water-level view from the Paul's Boat Lines tour (see pages 88-89) or you can head to the Dow's Lake Pavilion (OC Transpo route 3 to Preston Street and Prince of Wales Drive) and rent a pedal-boat. A two-person boat costs $11 per $\frac{1}{2}$ hour; a four-person craft is $13. Pedal-boating is hard work, so you'll find that 30 minutes is plenty of time to explore the banks of the arboretum or watch powerboats entering or leaving Hartwells Locks.

For many years, the canal's use was limited to the months between mid-spring and early fall. In 1969, civic leader Douglas Fullerton hit on the idea of turning the 7.8-kilometre (5-mile) section between Sapper's Bridge and Hartwells Locks into the **world's longest skating rink**. Now, on winter days, Dow's Lake and the canal are covered with thousands of skaters, ranging from toddlers on their first pair of bobskates to seniors. Since the condition of the ice surface is dependent on the weather, it's impossible to standardize opening and closing dates. On average, the rink is usually open by New Year's Day. Because of the high volume of traffic during Winterlude (see pages 130-31) and Ottawa's frequent late-winter thaws, the ice usually doesn't support skating past the end of February. You can call ahead for canal skating conditions at 232-1234.

The ice condition is indicated by red, yellow, or green flags flown at five main points on the rink: near the National Arts Centre, at the foot of Waverly Street, at Fifth Avenue, and at both ends of Dow's Lake. At each of these points there are heated buildings with skate rentals and areas to lace up your skates and store your footwear. Washrooms and several food concessions can be found there as well. Skating in cold weather really burns up the calories, so you can easily jus-

Skating on the Canal

tify indulging in two mainstays of canal rink-rats: poutine, a Québécois specialty of french-fried potatoes covered in gravy and cheese curds; and beavertails, rolled deep-fried bread dough covered in sugar.

If your family doesn't have skates, you can rent them inside the Dow's Lake Pavilion or at any of the skate-change buildings on the ice: adults, $6 per hour, maximum $25;

children under 13, $3 per hour to a maximum of $12. Baby sleighs and blankets are $6 per hour to a maximum of $25. For any rental, a $50 deposit or credit-card imprint is required. There's no charge to skate on the canal, but the National Capital Commission invites donations to help pay for upkeep. Donation boxes are located at each of the five skate-change locations.

5: In the steps of history

Since its elevation from lumbertown to government town, Ottawa has developed a split personality. Official duties lend it the stately air that for years branded it as a drab, conservative city. Yet it continues to show its roots as a rough-hewn pioneer outpost. The two personas coexist comfortably, though, making it unique among the world's capital cities. Scattered throughout the region are museums, monuments, and other attractions that reveal both sides of Ottawa's character.

Bank of Canada Currency Museum 🎏

Where? 245 Sparks Street (2 minutes' walk from Parliament Hill) 782-8914
When? May 1 to Labour Day, Mondays–Saturdays 10:30 am–5 pm; Labour Day to April 30, Tuesdays–Saturdays 10:30 am–5 pm
How much? $5 for families, $2 per person, children under 8 free; free admission on Tuesdays
How long? At least 1 hour
Extras: Fully wheelchair and stroller accessible

If you have ever entertained the fantasy of being Scrooge McDuck, Donald Duck's rich uncle who spent his time sitting in a vault full of dough, you'll enjoy visiting Scrooge's idea of heaven. Inside the Bank of Canada building on the western section of the Sparks Street Mall (a four-block-long pedestrian mall) is the Currency Museum. Seven galleries contain portions of the national currency collection, the world's most complete collection of Canadian notes and coins. There is also history in good measure, tracing the development of money over the past 2500 years. On view are examples of the shells, glass beads, teeth, and playing cards that have been used as currency in various cultures, and displays that show how coins are struck and banknotes printed.

Billings Estate Museum

Where? 2100 Cabot Street
247-4830
Transit: OC Transpo route 1 to Billings Bridge Plaza Shopping Centre, then walk east on Riverside Drive and follow the signs
When? May 1 to October 31, Sundays–Thursdays noon–5 pm
How much? Adults $2, seniors $1.50, children 5–18 $1, under 5 free
How long? 1/2 hour
Extras: Gift shop, main floor only accessible to wheelchairs and strollers, free parking

In 1813, Bradish and Lamira Billings were the first white settlers to build south of the Rideau River. The elegant frame house they constructed in 1828 has become a landmark in Ottawa's quiet Alta Vista neighbourhood. In addition to displaying artifacts from the Billingses' era, the museum stages exhibits depicting Ottawa's past. Various concerts and other events are held on the grounds of the estate. Aimed more at adults than at children, the museum warrants a brief visit if you're in the area.

Bytown Museum

Where? On the Rideau Canal at the foot of Parliament Hill
234-4570
When? May 1 to Thanksgiving, Mondays–Saturdays 10 am–5 pm, Sundays 1 pm–5 pm; Thanksgiving to November 30, Mondays–Fridays 10 am–4 pm; December 1 to March 31, weekdays by appointment 8 am–4 pm; April, weekdays 10 am–4 pm
How much? $6 for families, $2.50 for adults, $1.25 for

The Bytown Museum

students over 11, 50¢ for children under 12, free admission Sundays May 1 to Thanksgiving
How long? 1 hour
Extras: No wheelchair or stroller access to third floor, disabled parking only, postcards and historical books for sale

On the west bank of the Rideau Canal's Ottawa Locks below Parliament Hill, the Bytown Museum has one of the city's prime locations. The stone building is the oldest in Ottawa, erected to hold food and equipment for the men who built the canal. Appropriately, the contents focus on the canal's early years and on life in the town that grew up around it. There are Victorian clothes on mannequins, a period kitchen, and a doll collection. Despite its prominence — both in location and in tourist brochures — the Bytown is worth only a brief visit; the static displays won't hold kids' interest for long.

Canadian Museum of Contemporary Photography

Where? 1 Rideau Canal, entrance on the west wall of the Château Laurier Hotel 990-8257
Internet: http://www.chin. gc.ca/CHIN/CHINIndex/

The Canadian Museum of Contemporary Photography

Homepage/ngc/cmcp/english/en-cmcp.html
Transit: OC Transpo routes 2, 7, 14, and 18
When? May 1 to Thanksgiving, Mondays, Tuesdays, Fridays–Sundays
11 am–5 pm, Wednesdays 4–8 pm, closed Thursdays; Thanksgiving to April 30, Wednesdays, Fridays–Sundays 11 am–5 pm, Thursdays 11 am–8 pm, closed Mondays and Tuesdays
How much? Free
How long? 1 hour
Extras: Bookstore and boutique, fully wheelchair and stroller accessible, strollers available

Built in the tunnel that connected the Château Laurier Hotel to the old Union Station for more than 50 years, the Canadian Museum of Contemporary Photography — a division of the National Gallery of Canada — is Ottawa's newest museum. It's easy to miss the entrance if you're not aware that the museum hugs the western wall of the Château itself; the limestone exterior and balustrades are designed to blend into what was already there.

Inside, the use of light is ingenious, as befits a museum devoted to the art of manipulating light. The display space

71

is not large, but it suits the types of shows the museum has been mounting. There is also a 50-seat auditorium, and a research centre that the public can use by appointment.

Kids can try solving the mystery of a "feely box" by matching the identity of an object hidden inside a box with photographs on a wall. The boxes are available at the information desk.

With more than 1100 titles, the bookstore will entrance any shutterbug in your family, and the boutique has a good selection of posters and picture frames. It is also *the* best place to buy postcards in the city.

Canadian Police College (RCMP) Musical Ride ✱

Where? St. Laurent Boulevard and Sandridge Road
998-0754
Transit: OC Transpo route 7 to the front gate
When? Stables: weekdays 8:30–11 am and 1–3 pm; call for practice schedule
How much? Free
How long? 1–1½ hours, depending on what program is being rehearsed
Extras: No wheelchair or stroller access to stables, limited free parking

Since 1878, the Royal Canadian Mounted Police has been thrilling audiences around the world with its precision musical ride, a program that combines equestrian dressage, military pageantry, and a touch of Old West daredeviltry. All that precision takes practice, which is what you can find the team members doing when they're not on the road somewhere. Depending on when you go, you might see newer riders learning the routines or more seasoned riders brushing up on the tricky lance drill. The public is welcome at these rehearsals, but you must call ahead to determine the schedule. The team travels during the spring and summer, so the best time to catch a rehearsal is between late January and late April. Even when the main unit is away, you can visit the uniformly gorgeous RCMP horses in their stables.

The Royal Canadian Mounted Police Musical Ride

Canadian Ski Museum

Where? 457A Sussex Drive, between Murray and Clarence Streets (5 minutes' walk east of Parliament Hill) 241-5832

When? Tuesdays–Fridays noon–4 pm

How much? Adults $1, children 10–12 50¢, under 10 free

How long? ½ hour

Extras: Not accessible to wheelchairs or strollers, some posters are on sale

From cross-country pioneer Jackrabbit Johannsen to downhill champion Kate Pace-Lindsay, Canada has been home to many of the world's best skiers. A small diversion on the western edge of the Byward Market, the Canadian Ski Museum traces the origins of the sport all the way back to 3000 B.C. If your kids are ski or snowboard enthusiasts, they'll get a kick out of how technology has evolved since humans first put boards to snow.

Canadian War Museum

Where? 330 Sussex Drive, next to the National Gallery of Canada 776-8600

Internet: http://www.cmcc.muse.digital.ca/cwm/cwmeng/cwmeng.html

Transit: OC Transpo route 3

When? Victoria Day to

The Canadian War Museum

Thanksgiving, daily 9:30 am–5 pm, Thursdays 9:30 am–8 pm; Thanksgiving to Victoria Day, same, except closed Mondays
How much? $8 for families, $3.50 for adults, $2 for seniors and youth 13–17, $1 for children 6–12, children under 6 free; Canadian veterans and their guests free; free admission to all Thursdays 5–8 pm
How long? No less than 2 hours
Extras: Gift shop with a selection of military-related items, partially wheelchair and stroller accessible, diaper-changing facilities in one women's washroom, guided tours can be arranged if you book ahead

From its participation in the Boer War, under British command, to its back-up role in the Gulf War, Canada has had a long and proud military tradition. As noted in Chapter 2, it was a military action in World War I that signalled to the world that Canada had come into its own as a nation. The Canadian War Museum does a remarkable job of communicating a difficult message to visitors too young to have experienced war. The museum aims to display the artifacts of Canada's wars, commemorate the loss of thousands of lives, yet promote the concept of remembrance — the idea that only by remembering the past can society avoid repeating the same mistakes. Of course, some kids will just want to climb on the big Sherman tank outside the front door, but the museum's message does seem to sink in.

Remarkably, the war museum manages to hold kids' attention without many modern gadgets. Hands-on here means trying on vintage uniforms or testing out a World War I gas mask. There is a realistic re-creation of a First War trench, a mock-up of a mechanic working on the engine of a Spitfire, and numerous dioramas. In the summer, interpretive guides are on hand, and actors stage skits that bring history to life. And if you have trouble naming some Canadian heroes other than multimillionaire hockey players, be sure to visit the second-floor **Hall of Honour**, which commemorates 40 Canadians whose bravery won them their country's highest awards.

Laurier House National Historic Site

Where? 335 Laurier Avenue East
692-2581
Transit: OC Transpo route 316 to Laurier Avenue East and Chapel Street
When? April 1 to September 30, Tuesdays–Saturdays 9 am–5 pm, Sundays 2–5 pm, closed Mondays; October 1 to March 31, Tuesdays–Saturdays 10 am–5 pm, Sundays 2–5 pm, closed Mondays
How much? Adults $2.25, seniors and students over 16 $1.75, children 6–16 $1.25, children under 6 free
How long? 1 hour
Extras: Wheelchair access to main floor only

The stately brick home with the distinctive mansard roof and green pinstriped awnings has been a Sandy Hill landmark since its construction in 1878. The three-storey house was built by local jeweller John Leslie, who lived there until he sold it to the Liberal Party of Canada in 1896. The purchase price — $9500 — hardly

Laurier House

reflects the role the house has played in Canada's history.

Although the house was purchased as the official residence for Prime Minister Wilfrid Laurier and his wife, Zoe, the Liberal Party retained ownership, so the Lauriers continued to live there even after Wilfrid was defeated by Conservative Robert Borden in 1911. Indeed, Zoe stayed on alone after her husband died in 1919. When she died in 1921, the house was given to William Lyon Mackenzie King, Laurier's successor as leader of the Liberal Party. King willed it to Canada when he died in 1950, and it was opened to the public the following year. In 1957, the house was officially declared a national historic site.

It was King, the man who would dominate Canadian politics in the first half of this century as prime minister for 22 years, who named the residence Laurier House. He moved into the building in 1923, after considerable renovations had been completed. The most significant change was the addition of an elegant study on the third floor. As his diaries have shown, it was from this room that King determined the direction for Canada throughout the Depression and World War II. The fact that he reached decisions by conferring with his late mother and his pet dog makes King as fascinating a political figure as Canada has ever had.

King always considered himself Laurier's spiritual son — a meaningful designation considering his belief in the afterworld — so it's appropriate that several rooms on the second floor capture his predecessor's era with period furnishings and personal effects. A later prime minister, Lester Pearson, is also honoured with a re-creation of his study on the second floor. The room contains all the books, furnishings, and memorabilia from Pearson's original study, including his Nobel Peace Prize, awarded in 1957.

Two third-floor artifacts from King's era should not be overlooked: a portrait of his mother and his crystal ball. Also fascinating are the guest book, which contains the signatures of Sir Winston Churchill, Franklin Roosevelt, Charles de Gaulle, and child actress Shirley Temple, and a plaster cast of Abraham Lincoln's face.

Logan Hall/ Geological Survey of Canada

Where? 601 Booth Street 995-4261
Transit: OC Transpo route 6 to Carling Avenue and Booth Street
When? Weekdays 8 am– 4 pm
How much? Free
How long? $1/2$ hour
Extras: Fully wheelchair and stroller accessible

Slightly off the beaten tourist track, Logan Hall is a rockhound's paradise. The Geological Survey of Canada, founded in 1842, has played an integral role in helping to open up this country's frontiers in the west and the Arctic. The work of its first director, William Logan, helped determine the path of the railroad to the Pacific, and his team mapped out much of the new land.

Logan Hall contains a sampling of the organization's 60,000 minerals and gems, which include crystals, volcanic rocks, and a number of species that have been named for Canadian geologists. Also on display is part of Canada's collection of meteorites, a large number of fossils, and examples of prospectors' tools and equipment.

Architectural ruins at the Mackenzie King Estate

Mackenzie King Estate ✱

Where? In Gatineau Park, 72 Barnes Road, off Gatineau Parkway in Chelsea, Quebec, a 25-minute drive north of downtown 239-5000 or 1-800-465-1867
When? Victoria Day to mid-June, Wednesdays–Sundays noon–5 pm; mid-June to Thanksgiving, daily noon–5 pm; closed Thanksgiving to Victoria Day
How much? $6 per car, including parking

How long? 2–3 hours
Extras: Snackbar, tea room, picnics are not permitted, partially wheelchair and stroller accessible, dogs are allowed if on leash

This is the kind of place that makes Canadian history come alive for school-age children. Combining the unique personality of the nation's 10th prime minister (see Laurier House, pages 75–77) with enough countryside for any kid to run off some energy, the Mackenzie King Estate is one of the jewels of **Gatineau Park** (see pages 109–10).

King was 25 when he biked into the hills north of Ottawa on Thanksgiving Day 1900. What he saw there, on a day when the forest was probably radiant with orange and red foliage, ignited a love affair with the area that lasted until his death 50 years later. The young civil servant began buying up property near Kingsmere Lake; eventually he would own 231 hectares (570 acres) south of the lake, including a large summer house he called **Moorside**. In 1927, he added a 19th-century pioneer house called **the Farm**, which became his full-time restoration project after his retirement in 1948.

King planted trees from around the world at Moorside, and also used the property to indulge his fascination with architecture. He bought his first ruin — part of an old Ottawa house — in 1935, and arranged it artfully on the grounds. His collection grew to include pieces from the original Centre Block, fragments from the British Houses of Parliament, and a doorway and windows from Ottawa's Bank of North America. There's something in King's obsession with interesting but essentially worthless pieces of stone that kids relate to. The large pillars and stone arches also allow youngsters to indulge their fantasies of medieval knights and ladies.

Several parts of the estate are closed to the public — including the Farm, which is the official residence of the Speaker of the House of Commons — but the original Kingswood and Moorside cottages have been restored to the way they looked when King lived in them. You can also visit the **outdoor abbey** that King constructed with his ruins, the boat house where his beloved mother lived until 1917, and his formal gardens. Films depicting various events in King's life are shown in two of the estate's garages.

Picnicking is not allowed on the grounds, but you can buy a light lunch at the Moorside Tea Room.

The Moorside Tea Room at the Mackenzie King Estate

National Library and National Archives of Canada

Where? 395 Wellington
Street, 5 blocks west
of Parliament Hill
National Archives 995-5138
National Library 992-9988
When? Exhibition area:
daily 9 am–9 pm
How much? Free
How long? 1 hour
Extras: Fully wheelchair
and stroller accessible,
limited free parking

Canada's desire to archive its historical documents dates back almost as far as the country itself. Formed in 1872, the National Archives is the nation's oldest cultural institution. Although the archives were started just after Confederation, it wasn't until Arthur Doughty was appointed Dominion Archivist in 1903 that the collection really began to grow. Today, the archives hold more than 60 million manuscripts and government records, as well as millions of maps and architectural drawings. A statue of Doughty stands behind the rather imposing National Library/National Archives Building, overlooking the river and the Quebec hills beyond.

The National Library is a much younger institution, founded in 1952, but it has more of a public face. While the archives are used mainly by researchers and writers, the library holds a number of public programs, including readings by Canadian authors, film screenings, and a popular series of jazz concerts.

Exhibits by either of these historical branches tend to be rather low-key, but often they contain intriguing pieces of our history. Occasionally an exhibit like the 1995 look at science fiction will have more kid-appeal than you might expect from a national library and archives. If you have a young musician with you, don't miss Glenn Gould's massive black Steinway, which is located near the staircase on the main floor when it's not in use for a concert in the auditorium.

National War Memorial

The large granite arch of the War Memorial, topped by a winged figure, is one of

The National War Memorial

Ottawa's most recognizable landmarks. Situated in the middle of **Confederation Square**, between the Rideau Canal and Parliament Hill, it is visible for blocks in several directions. The monument was built to commemorate the sac-rifices of Canada's military in World War I, and unveiled by King George VI on May 21, 1939. Since then, the cenotaph has been updated to reflect Canada's losses in World War II and the Korean War, and renovated several times by the

Royal Canadian Legion. Most recently, the 22 figures at the centre of the monument have been cleaned thoroughly, renewing features that had been obscured by years of air pollution and bird excrement. The monument is beautifully illuminated at night.

Nepean Museum

Where? 16 Rowley Avenue, Nepean, 2 blocks north of Meadowlands Drive
723-7936
Transit: OC Transpo route 86 to Meadowlands Drive and Rowley Avenue
When? Tuesdays–Saturdays 10 am–4 pm, Sundays 1–4 pm
How much? Free
How long? 1 hour
Extras: Small gift shop, fully wheelchair and stroller accessible, free parking

In 1793, seven years before Philemon Wright built his sawmill at Hull (see page 15), surveyors were at work well south of the Ottawa, in the employ of George Hamilton, an Irish veteran of the American Revolution. Nothing came of Hamilton's plans to settle on the Rideau, but his early claim is the basis for an argument the City of Nepean makes for pre-dating Ottawa proper.

Don't expect any bells or whistles at the tiny Nepean Museum — you're more likely to find an elderly resident's extensive collection of teddy bears. Rather, it's a refreshing reminder of the area's not-so-distant rural past. It's worth a quick visit if you've taken the kids to the nearby Gym Jam (see page 122) or the Canadian Wildlife Federation Gift Gallery (see page 92).

Nepean Point

One of the best views of Ottawa, Hull, and the Gatineau Hills is from Nepean Point, a rocky hill overlooking the Ottawa River a few minutes' walk west of the National Gallery of Canada. Dominating the hill is a statue of French explorer Samuel de Champlain, who is depicted taking a navigational reading with the astrolabe he is storied to have lost near this spot in 1613. The side of the hill forms a natural amphitheatre, called the **Astrolabe Theatre**, naturally enough. Built for Canada's centennial in 1967, it is the site of many types of concerts throughout the summer. (See local newspapers to find out what's on.) On a warm evening with the moon rising behind the Peace Tower, it is one of the most beautiful music venues imaginable.

Ottawa Art Gallery

Where? 2 Daly Avenue, at Nicholas Street
233-8699
Transit: OC Transpo route 5
When? Tuesdays–Fridays 10 am–5 pm, Thursdays 10 am–8 pm, Saturdays and Sundays noon–5 pm
How much? Free
How long? 1–2 hours
Extras: Fully wheelchair and stroller accessible

Housed in **Arts Court**, the city's first courthouse before its conversion, the gallery features rotating exhibits by some of the area's finest artists, and some from outside the region. Also on display are a number of works, including some early sketches, by members of the Group of Seven. These are part of the collection of the late O.J. Firestone, a local businessman who had an eye for rising young talent.

Ottawa International Hostel

Where? 75 Nicholas Street
235-2595
Transit: OC Transpo route 5
When? Tours by appointment only
How much? Free
How long? 1 hour
Extras: Limited access for wheelchairs and strollers

You may not have stayed in a youth hostel since you backpacked through Europe, but this one is worth a visit. For over a century the building was Ottawa's jail, and although the locks have been removed the cell doors remain. The tour highlights many interesting facets of the old building, including the scene of Canada's last public hanging.

Rideau Hall

Where? 1 Sussex Drive, at northwestern edge of Rockcliffe Village
998-7113 or 1-800-465-6890
Transit: OC Transpo route 3 to front gates
When? Walking tours of the grounds are conducted at

various times most days throughout the year, but between November and March the tours are on weekends by appointment only; tours of the residence's public rooms are conducted on weekends during July and August
How much? Free
How long? 1–2 hours
Extras: Fully wheelchair and stroller accessible

Built in 1838 by lumber baron Thomas MacKay, the official residence of the Governor General, the Queen's representative in Canada, is situated on beautiful grounds that are lovingly cared for by some of the country's best gardeners. Tours of the gardens and arboretum leave from the front gate, where, during the summer, you can watch a Changing the Guard ceremony at the top of every hour, 10 am–6 pm. Access to the splendid public rooms of the house is more limited. Organizations are permitted to tour parts of Rideau Hall by appointment on weekdays; individuals can take a tour of the public rooms on weekends in July and August.

Royal Canadian Mint ✱

Where? 320 Sussex Drive, north of National Gallery of Canada
993-8990
Internet: http://www.rcmint.ca
Transit: OC Transpo route 3
When? Tours by appointment only, weekdays May 1– September 1
How much? $2 per person, children under 6 free
How long? 1 hour
Extras: Fully wheelchair and stroller accessible; the Mint's boutique sells a variety of collector coins

A visit to the Royal Canadian Mint makes the perfect companion to a trip to the Bank of Canada Currency Museum. Open since 1908, the mint has established a worldwide reputation as one of the most versatile manufacturers of coins, medals, and tokens. Although Canada's circulation coinage is now produced at the mint's branch operation in Winnipeg, at the Ottawa plant you can watch production of silver, gold, and platinum Maple Leaf bullion coins and

Rideau Hall, official residence of the Governor General

specialty products for foreign countries. This is one of the oldest and largest gold refineries in the Western world.

Security is obviously very tight at the Mint, and your tour is strictly controlled, but it's a fascinating process to watch even if you can't touch. The closest you'll get to all that loot is ogling the display of $1 million in pure gold bars in the boutique.

Strathcona Park

Transit: OC Transpo route 5 to Laurier Avenue and Charlotte Street

At the east end of historic Laurier Avenue East, Strathcona Park offers a number of diversions, just as it has since the days when the children of Ottawa's founders played there. Highlighted by a large fountain, paved paths, children's wading pool, and playground, the park stretches for several blocks along the west bank of the Rideau River. Range Road, which borders the park and runs south down a steep hill from Laurier Avenue, is the site of several foreign embassies and high commissions. In the evenings, young people from many countries gather in the park to play soccer. In the summer, the Odyssey Theatre Company takes up residence in the park to stage performances under the stars. Information on their performances is available at 232-8407.

6: Seeing the city from street, water, and sky

ou can explore Ottawa from a huge variety of means of transport, including your own feet. Whether your brood has history buffs, architecture fans, nature nuts, or environment enthusiasts, Ottawa has a tour for each of them. Try the three neighbourhood tours in this chapter for a glimpse of the Ottawa that visitors rarely see.

Commercial tours

Aircraft tours

Based on the Ottawa River in Gatineau, Quebec, **Air Outaouais** (819-568-2359) offers seaplane excursions for up to five passengers. The flights range from a 15-minute circuit over Ottawa to day-long trips to historic Upper Canada Village on the St. Lawrence River or Montebello, northwest of Montreal. Rates begin at $35 for adults, $31.50 for seniors and students, and $17.50 for children. Family discounts are available. The airline operates in daylight hours May 1 to November 1.

The **Ottawa Flying Club** (523-2142), which operates out of the Macdonald-Cartier International Airport, can arrange a one-hour tour of the city at any time of the year, provided you give them several days' notice. Rates vary but average about $30 per person.

Balloon tours

Hot air ballooning is very popular in Ottawa, and it's not unusual to see two or three balloons hanging on the horizon if the winds are calm. It's not a cheap way to fly, but it provides an unparalleled view of the ground below. The key thing to remember about ballooning is that you literally have to go with the flow. Takeoff and landing points and flight itineraries are dependent on wind direction and speed. Balloons are permitted to fly only between two hours after sunrise and two hours before sunset.

Ballons Richer (228-7431) offers year-round flights, weather permitting, that last 2–3 hours from inflation to touchdown. Flights usually leave from LeBreton Flats, just west of the downtown core. Adults can enjoy the traditional champagne aloft, while children can sip soft drinks. Every passenger receives a pin and pictures of the flight as souvenirs. The cost is $150 for adults, $100 for children over 10 years but below 45 kilograms (100 pounds), $75 for children 5–10; children under 5 fly free. You should book your flight several days in advance.

Skyview Ballooning (724-7784) has two scheduled flights a day, and a pricing system that makes it considerably cheaper to fly on weekday mornings. A 90-minute morning flight between April 15 and November 15 costs $125 for adults and $107 for children under 13, while an evening excursion is $165 each. Winter rates are $59 per person in the mornings and $79 per person in the afternoons. Skyview also has a "fourth person flies free" policy that makes family flying more affordable. On winter flights, the traditional champagne is replaced with coffee and liqueur. Kids are served peach juice on summer flights. Book your flight one week in advance.

Windborne Ballooning (739-7388) offers the customary champagne or soft drinks and souvenir photo, and charges $150 per person or $275 a couple for a 90-minute flight. An in-flight commentary is provided by the pilot. It's recommended you reserve two or three weeks in advance for winter or summer weekend flights. One week's notice is sufficient for weekdays.

Bicycle tours

Ottawa is well suited to bicycle travel, but there's no need to haul your own spokes to town to enjoy some two-wheeling. Located on MacKenzie Avenue behind the Château Laurier Hotel from early April to late October, **Rent-a-Bike** (241-4140) carries nine models of bikes, including children's models and tandems. Other wheeled conveyances like in-line skates and kids' bicycle buggies are also available. The rate is $4 per hour to a maximum of $12, which includes a helmet, lock, and maps. A credit-card imprint is required as a deposit. A two-hour guided tour is $14 per person, and you must book it in advance. The rental stand opens at 9 am and closes one hour before sunset.

Boat tours

The *Bytown Pumper* is the last wood-burning steamship in North America, and a trip on board her is a unique experience. From mid-May to Thanksgiving, the *Pumper* plies the Rideau River from the Hog's Back Marina south to Black Rapids and back. The trip takes two hours and departs on weekends and holiday Mondays at 2 and 4 pm. Rates are $25 for a family, $10 for adults, $8 for seniors and students over 12, and $5 for children under 13. The *Pumper*

is licensed and also serves non-alcoholic beverages. Reservations are required; phone 736-9893.

The *Sea Prince II* belonging to the **Ottawa Riverboat Company** (562-4888) ferries passengers along the Ottawa from May 1 to Thanksgiving. The boat makes six 90-minute trips a day beginning at 10:30 am. The last cruise sets out at 6:45 pm. A prerecorded narration is provided. The fare is $30 for a family, $12 for adults, $9 for seniors and students over 12, $6 for children 6–12; children under 6 are free. Tickets can be purchased on Sapper's Bridge at Confederation Square.

Paul's Boat Lines (225-6781) was one of the first companies

The Bytown Pumper

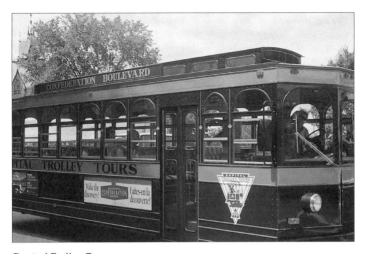

Capital Trolley Tours

to cater to tourists in Ottawa, and its narrated excursions on the Rideau Canal and Ottawa River continue to pack them in. The boats operate from mid-May to Thanksgiving, and the company's large fleet ensures that there is almost always a tour ready to leave when you are. Tickets can be purchased at the company's kiosk on Sapper's Bridge at Confederation Square. The fare is $30 for a family, $12 for adults, $10 for seniors and students over 11, $6 for children 5–11; children under 5 are free. The canal cruise takes 75 minutes and runs 10 am–8:30 pm; the river excursion lasts 90 minutes and operates 11 am–7:30 pm.

Bus tours
Capital Trolley Tours

(729-6888) operates two-hour narrated tours of Ottawa on a reproduction of a 1940 electric trolleybus, making 15 stops along its route. You can get on or off at any point throughout the day. From the beginning of May to the end of October, the buses run every ½ hour, leaving Confederation Square 10 am–4 pm. During the rest of the year, they run on weekends 7–9 pm. The fare is $46 for a family, $16 for adults, $13 for seniors and students over 15, $9 for children 5–15; children under 5 ride free. Tickets can be purchased on the bus or at the Info Ottawa kiosk at the corner

Piccadilly Bus Tours

of Sparks and Elgin Streets. Discounts are offered for some museums and restaurants.

From mid-May to mid-October, **Gray Line of Ottawa** (725-1441) offers a 2½-hour narrated tour of the capital that includes commentary on 15 of the major attractions in the core. Photo stops are made at Notre-Dame Basilica, Rockcliffe Park, Rideau Falls, and the Central Experimental Farm. In May, June, September, and October, the tours leave Confederation Square at 9:30 am and 1:30 pm; during the summer, tours depart hourly 9:30–11:30 am, and at 1:30 and 2:30 pm. Fares are $42 for a family of four, $16 for

adults, $14 for seniors, and $9 for children 5–12; children under 5 ride free.

Gray Line also offers package tours that combine the scenic bus route above with tours of the Canadian Museum of Civilization and Rideau Hall, a Rideau Canal cruise, or a steam train trip to Wakefield, Quebec (see pages 110-11). While convenient, these packages do not offer good value. For example, a family of four could take the bus and train tours separately for $110; Gray Line's package price is $140.

Better value is offered on board one of the red double-deckers of **Piccadilly Bus Tours** (820-6745). The authentic

London buses tool around on two-hour circuits, but you can get on or off at any of 10 different attractions. Piccadilly covers the most territory of any of the bus tours, ranging from Rockcliffe Park in the east to Island Park Drive in the city's west end. The narrated tours are offered from the beginning of May to the end of October. There are up to nine departures in the peak season, with two or three daily departures in the shoulder seasons. Throughout the season, the first bus leaves at 10:30 am; the last bus departs at 4:30 pm during most of the season. The tours start from Confederation Square, but you can board anywhere along the route. Fares are $42 for families, $15 for adults, $11 for seniors and students over 15, $7 for children under 16.

Rickshaw tours

For a very different view of the city, **Orient Express Rickshaws** (797-9980) lets you direct your personal driver and determine your own route. The drivers are muscular college students, and half the fun of the tour is watching them work their way through traffic. The service runs May 1 to mid-September, and rates are flexible. You can negotiate with the driver before you set out, or establish a maximum and go on what amounts to a magical mystery tour. The average price for a tour of the Byward Market is $10–$20, depending on how much you want to cover. The rickshaws are based in the Market but don't have a permanent station, so you can hail a driver if you see one running by. Although they are built to hold two adults, an adult and two small children could also ride comfortably.

Theme tours
Ottawa Valley Field Trips

(820-1943) offers many bus and walking excursions, including shopping tours to Montreal and New York State; locally, they organize trips to several rural areas and specialize in taking visitors to lesser-known attractions. Nature walks are one of the company's specialties. Prices for the local tours range from $25 to $50 for people over 11, and half-fare for children under 12.

For those looking for something beyond the usual fare,

Specialty shops for kids

In addition to those stores of special interest to kids highlighted in the neighbourhood tours, there are a number of others you might want to include in your Ottawa itinerary.

The Bookery at 541 Sussex Drive, 241-1428, has been an institution at the western edge of the Byward Market for years. It carries a huge stock of children's books in English and French, as well as art prints, tapes, and videos. Long before large book chains introduced chairs into their stores, the Bookery provided cosy nooks for curling up to examine a potential purchase.

Canada's Four Corners: Since the 1960s, this store has had the city's largest selection of Canadian handicrafts, Inuit carvings, and native art. There are also handmade sweaters, pottery, jewellery, and the ubiquitous Mountie and beaver souvenirs. 93 Sparks Street, 233-2322.

Canadian Wildlife Federation Gift Gallery: Located in suburban Nepean at 1558 Merivale Road, 225-6322, this store is off the usual tourist track but well worth a visit if you have a child with an interest in wild animals and birds. The store has a wide array of books, recordings, and clothing with nature themes, as well as smaller items like keychains and bookmarks that make great souvenirs or gifts for friends back home.

Folio: If you're looking for a unique souvenir or just want to browse among some unusual items, this store, a long-time fixture on Bank Street, is the place to go. It carries an assortment of stationery, toys, books, and lamps, many from European designers. Kids will love kitschy items like a Mickey Mouse tea service and the kooky cookie jars. Now in the Byward Market at 459 Sussex Drive, 241-6336.

Kid's Cosy Cottons: As the name suggests, the shop

specializes in children's cotton clothing, both knitted and woven. The store's designers focus on practical clothing with colours and patterns that kids love. The sizes range from newborns to 12 years, and the company also has a mail-order catalogue that you can take home with you. 517 Sussex Drive, 562-2679.

Lilliput: Miniatures hold a special fascination for children of all ages, including some grown-ups with fond memories of toy soldiers or handmade dollhouses. Lilliput handles a full line of tiny household furnishings, as well as well-designed dollhouse kits in a variety of styles. 9 Murray Street, 241-1183.

The Scout Shop Camping Centre: If there's a Scout in your family, then Scouts Canada headquarters, distinguished by its weathered totem pole, is probably a must-see that ranks right up there with Parliament Hill. Located at 1345 Baseline Road, 224-0139, the camping centre carries all the official Scouting gear and uniform paraphernalia.

The Snow Goose: Native Canadian handicrafts remain among the most expressive symbols of our country, and the Snow Goose doubles as a gallery of both fine artwork and practical items. Our kids used to be addicted to the wonderfully furry rabbit slippers, and never left the store without examining the selection of fine silver earrings. 83 Sparks Street, 232-2213.

Scouts Canada Headquarters

Adventure Playground Tours
(238-2058) provides a wide range of options. You can explore nature and eat a native feast of bannock, moose, and beaver, tour artists' galleries, spend a day with a golf pro, or take part in a murder mystery in a heritage building. Prices range up to $300 per person. Advance booking is a must.

Walking tours

Ottawa is a great city for walking. Its compact size makes it possible to see many of its major attractions without ever leaving your feet. Several commercial operators offer packages that provide guides and/or maps, depending on your preference.

Ottawa On Foot Tours
(230-5229) offers regularly scheduled walks through Ottawa's historic neighbourhoods from early May to mid-October, but tours at other times of the year can also be arranged. Tickets can be purchased in the courtyard at the corner of Metcalfe and Wellington Streets. $10 for adults, $7 for seniors and students, $4 for children.

Ottawa Walks (744-4307) presents a choice of nine tours,

including ones on Ottawa's literary history and the city's historic statues. By appointment only from May 20 to October 31. $6 for adults, $5 for seniors and students, preschoolers are free.

Three tours of Ottawa neighbourhoods

Guided tours can be fun, but sometimes it's more interesting to explore on your own, at your own pace. We've designed three tours, two bicycle tours and one walking circuit, that take you into our favourite neighbourhoods. All three travel on a mixture of commercial and residential streets, using both streets and bike paths. Each will give you the flavour of these historic areas — all have very different characters — but don't be afraid to wander off the suggested routes.

Bicycle tour #1: New Edinburgh/ Rockcliffe Park

Where? Between Beechwood Avenue and Sussex Drive, east of the

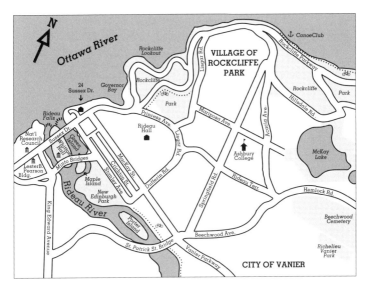

Bike Tour # 1

Rideau River
Start/Finish: At Beechwood Avenue and Crichton Street, a 10-minute ride from Parliament Hill
How long? 1–2 hours

The intersection of Beechwood Avenue and Crichton Street is the northwest corner of a small city-within-a-city called Vanier, after former governor general Georges Vanier. The first leg of this tour takes you through the old, toney Ottawa neighbourhood of New Edinburgh; the second half carries you into Rockcliffe Park, a separately incorporated village and home to

many diplomats, politicians, and successful business executives.

Depending on the time of day, the weather, and the state of family members' stomachs, you can choose to defer lunch until the end of the tour, or take along a picnic spread. If you prefer the latter option, make your first stop **Ryley & Maclachlan Fine Caterers** at 419 MacKay Street, which offers wonderful carry-out fare in addition to its banquet ser vices. If you're bringing your own sandwich fillings with you, you might prefer picking up some delicious fresh bread around the corner at **Bread &**

95

Roses Bakery, 11 Beechwood Avenue.

You would be hard pressed to begin a bicycle tour at a more appropriate place than **Mountain Equipment Co-op** at 5B Beechwood Avenue and Crichton Street. Part of a national chain of member-owned outfitters, the store has a huge stock of clothing and accessories for any outdoor activity from biking to mountain climbing. The first time you make a purchase at Mountain Equipment Co-op, you must also buy a membership for $5, which gives you voting privileges and catalogue service.

Now that you've stocked up for your trip, head away from Beechwood Avenue on Crichton Street. Turn left on Dufferin Road and continue around the corner, where it becomes Stanley Avenue. On your left is the beautiful **New Edinburgh Park**, which juts into the mouth of the Rideau River. If you've brought along your lunch, this is a fine place to enjoy it.

Follow Stanley Avenue until it branches left across the river on the double spans of the Minto Bridges. The centre link of the bridges is Green Island, site of **Whitton Hall**, Ottawa's city hall since 1958. Originally a small, boxy structure, the building recently received a significant facelift by renowned architect Moshe Safdie. While not as visually stunning as Safdie's National Gallery of Canada, it is nonetheless a bold design that leaves no room for middle-ground opinion. If you want to see the inside of the building, it's open to the public weekdays 8:30 am–4:30 pm (4 pm in the summer) and often features displays by local artists. Tours are available by appointment (244-5464). City Hall also makes a good bathroom break if you've spent some time enjoying New Edinburgh Park.

In front of you at the end of the Minto Bridges is the Lester B. Pearson Building, the headquarters of Foreign Affairs Canada. The roads surrounding the building offer several options for heading right, out to Sussex Drive. Cross Sussex, noting the stately headquarters of Canada's National Research Council opposite the Pearson complex.

To the right of the NRC is a small park that overlooks

Whitton Hall, Ottawa's city hall

Rideau Falls, where the Rideau River tumbles into the Ottawa River. French explorer Samuel de Champlain and his crew named the falls "rideau" because the falling water resembles sheer curtains. In the park is a fascinating sculpture by Stephen Brathwaite. Erected in 1992 to celebrate Canada's 125th anniversary, *Shelter* incorporates glass masks of 50 Canadians from all walks of life who visited Ottawa that year from across the country.

Take Sussex Drive past the falls to the northern bank. Overlooking the falls is the Embassy of France, a striking house that arguably has the best location in the city. Adjacent to the embassy is 24 Sussex Drive, the official residence of Canada's prime minister. The house itself is hard to see from the gates, which seal it off from the public.

Much more interesting visually is Rideau Hall, directly across Sussex Drive (see pages 83-84). The Governor General's residence sits at the western boundary of the village of Rockcliffe Park, which you can enter by turning right onto Princess Avenue. Princess runs along the outside of the northern wall of Rideau Hall's grounds, giving you the opportunity to appreciate the work of some of the country's top landscapers.

Some of the houses in Rockcliffe Park are valued at several million dollars. Veer left off Princess onto Lisgar Road for a short distance and then right onto Mariposa Avenue,

97

At the gates to Rideau Hall

one of Rockcliffe's main streets. On the right, just past Springfield Road, is Ashbury College, a private school that has educated many Canadian upper-class scions. Formerly a boys' school, Ashbury now has a co-ed program.

If you haven't eaten your picnic yet, continue on Mariposa to the end, where it meets the small park surrounding pretty McKay Lake. Otherwise, turn right onto Acacia Avenue and follow it out of Rockcliffe Park back to Beechwood Avenue.

Gentrification has come quickly to Beechwood, and in the 1990s its businesses serve the lifestyles of the residents of New Edinburgh and Rockcliffe Park. Two trendy coffee bars are among the latest additions.

At **Second Cup**, 1 Springfield Road and Beechwood Avenue, or **Grabbajabba**, 35 Beechwood Avenue and MacKay Street, you can relax over caffè latte, moccaccino, or cappuccino. If fine coffees put you in the mood for dessert, be sure to drop into **Le Chocolat Belge-Daniel** at 411 MacKay Street, makers of fine chocolates and other goodies.

For something more substantial, check out the **New Edinburgh Pub** at 1 Beechwood Avenue and Crichton Street. Despite its name, the pub is a family-friendly neighbourhood restaurant with a children's menu and a slew of non-alcoholic drinks and juices, in addition to a wide selection of beers. Its rooftop patio is a fine place to spend a warm summer evening.

Before you leave the neighbourhood, stop at **Birders World Nature Store** at 2 Beechwood Avenue. The store has a good stock of nature books and accessories for eco-friendly shoppers.

Bicycle tour #2: Hintonburg/ Westboro

Where? Between the Portage Bridge and Churchill Avenue, south of the Ottawa River

Start/Finish: Wellington Street at the Portage Bridge, west of the National Library and Archives of Canada, a 2-minute ride from Parliament Hill

How long? 2–3 hours

Like many North American cities, Ottawa grew by subsuming smaller communities. Westboro was one of the last to join, retaining its status as a separate village well into the 20th century. Today, it continues to have the feel of a small town, and several generations have grown up on its streets. To reach it, head west on the Ottawa River Parkway bike path from the Portage Bridge at Wellington Street.

At the bottom of the first rise is Lemieux Island, site of one of the city's filtration plants, and a railroad bridge that has provided a link to the Quebec side of the river since the early 1900s. Take the Parkdale Avenue exit, just past Lemieux Island, and head south on Parkdale. On the right is a large group of office buildings, collectively known as Tunney's Pasture. A federal government enclave, this is the headquarters for Health Canada and Statistics Canada.

Continue on Parkdale past Scott Street to Armstrong Street and the **Parkdale Market**. This is a smaller version of the Byward Market, open daily, that has about a dozen stalls of fruit, vegetables, flowers, maple syrup, or Christmas trees, depending on the time of year. There is a small municipal park directly behind the market, where you can enjoy a rest and a snack.

Once you're revived, mount up and turn right off Parkdale onto Wellington Street. If you need some souvenirs of your visit but want something other than a plastic Mountie or

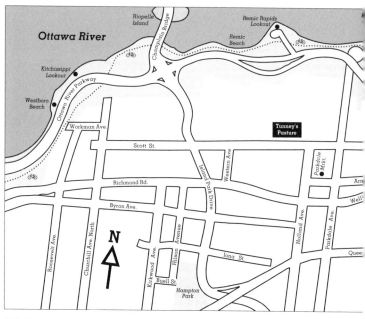

Bike Tour # 2

beaver, drop into **Crossroads** at 1242 Wellington Street. The shop carries a good selection of handmade crafts, including many items by local artisans.

Four blocks more will bring you to one of the city's lesser-known treasures, the **Ottawa Bagel Shop & Deli** at 1321 Wellington Street. For years, the only authentic, hand-rolled bagels in eastern Canada were available in Montreal's Plateau district. In the early '80s, the Bagel Shop & Deli brought in Ottawa's first wood-burning oven and a wealth of bagel-rolling experience learned first-hand in Montreal. The store has expanded several times and now stocks everything from gourmet chocolates to olive oil, but the woodstove remains the centrepoint. Kids love watching the raw dough cooking on long wooden boards. Free samples of various types are always available.

Directly across Wellington at no. 1308 is **Wellington Street News**, one of the city's better newsstands. The store has a good selection of U.S. and Canadian dailies, as well as many magazines and journals.

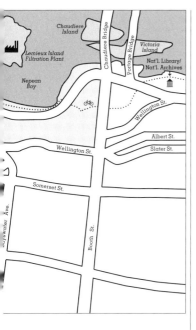

If you didn't indulge in the bagels and you're ready for lunch at this point, try **Devine's** at 15 Richmond Road (Wellington Street becomes Richmond at Western Avenue). The vegetarian restaurant specializes in main dishes like moussaka, lasagna, spinach pies, and tofu stir-fries, but lighter fare like muffins and yogurt is also available. On the weekend, a brunch features Belgian waffles, pancakes, and scrambled eggs.

If your family's tastes run to something less healthy but incredibly good, stay on your bikes for another two blocks, past Island Park Drive, until you reach the Canadian Tire store at 119 Richmond Road. Across the street most days will be a blue-and-yellow step-van with the name **Glen's** painted on the side. Year after year, Glen's has won various informal polls on Ottawa's best french fries. Ottawans take their street fries seriously. On any weekday, you'll see vans and buses parked on street corners throughout downtown Ottawa, cooking and selling fries. But Glen's is the best. His secret is very fresh peanut oil and only the best spuds available.

Whatever your choice of food, head south on Island Park Drive next. A federally owned parkway, the street has some stately stone houses and is home to several foreign missions and embassies. On your right, after you cross Byron Avenue, are the residence of the Mexican ambassador and the Embassy of Thailand.

Continue past Iona Street and turn right into Hampton Park. Dutch elm disease has destroyed many of the older

Public art smarts

The Terry Fox statue

As the national capital, Ottawa has become the home for hundreds of works of public art, ranging from the traditional statues on Parliament Hill to avant-garde works that people either love or hate. The power of some works — like the heroic larger-than-life figure of one-legged runner Terry Fox (at the southwest corner of Sussex Drive and Rideau Street) and Vernon March's towering National War Memorial — is indisputable. Others, like Art Price's fascinating *Tin House* wall hanging (in the courtyard at the corner of Clarence Street and Sussex Drive), blend into the streetscape so well that you could overlook them if you didn't know where to look. The National Capital Commission publishes an interesting guide, *street smART*, that will help you recognize and understand the various works of art you'll encounter while moving around the city. *street smART* is available free at the Info Ottawa kiosk at 101 Sparks Street or at Canada's Capital Information Centre, 14 Metcalfe Street.

Tin House

trees that once filled the park, but it remains a pleasant green space on a busy street. Head up the rise on the bike path and leave the park on a small street called Buell. Take the first right onto Hilson Avenue, then follow Hilson north across Byron Avenue back to Richmond Road.

Keep your eyes peeled at this point for a tall fellow with black hair and blue suede shoes, just in case you decide to pay a visit to the Official Elvis Sighting Society, which meets regularly at the **Newport Restaurant**, 334 Richmond Road. Popularized by a local sportswriter, the kitschy restaurant has more pictures of the King than any place north of Graceland, and serves great diner food, too.

If you have teenagers who are too cool by half for the Newport, try the **Nu Café** at 295 Richmond Road. They'll love the post-modern hanging lamps and purple walls; you'll love the terrific Mediterranean-style sandwiches that are the daily lunch special.

Depending on the weather and your time, you have two choices from here. You can head back downtown, or take time out for some sun and a swim. Either way, turn right from Richmond onto Churchill Avenue North. If you want to skip the beach, go straight on Churchill until you reach the Ottawa River Parkway bike path again and turn right for the return trip.

To reach the beach, turn left onto Workman Avenue, just past Scott Street, and follow it to the parkway and a path that goes under the road to the river. **Westboro Beach** has washrooms and change facilities and is supervised during the summer. (To check water quality, call 244-5678.)

Just east of and above the beach is the **Kitchissippi Lookout**, which provides a nice view of the Gatineau Hills.

Walking tour: The Glebe

Where? Between Clemow and Fifth Avenues, west of the Rideau Canal
Start/Finish: Elgin Street at the Pretoria Bridge, a 15-minute walk from Parliament Hill
How long? 1–2 hours

Webster's defines a glebe as "a plot of cultivated land." In Ottawa's early years, the neighbourhood known as the Glebe epitomized that definition; today, it sprouts houses and shops. During the last 30 years, the Glebe has become home to many successful professional couples and their children. Close to the Rideau Canal, several schools, and a thriving commercial street, the neighbourhood has a reputation for stressing the quality of life and for left-leaning activism. It also contains some of the finest examples of late Victorian architecture in the city.

The first leg of the tour — the Queen Elizabeth Driveway from the Pretoria Bridge to the **Canal Ritz Restaurant** — will cover familiar ground if you've been in town for a few days. We never tire of it, especially on spring days when the area is filled with joggers, in-line skaters, and parents taking their wintertime babies for their first extended pram rides. We also never tire of dessert and coffee at the Canal Ritz, nor of the great view it gives you of the canal.

If you can tear yourself away from the Ritz, head west on Fifth Avenue until you reach Bank Street. The corner of Fifth and Bank isn't exactly Times Square, but if you know people in Ottawa you *are* likely to see them here if you wait long enough.

The Papery, 850 Bank Street at Fifth, is heaven for anyone who has a fascination with things printed on or fashioned from paper. The store has a great selection of greeting cards and wrapping paper, and younger kids will love the range of stickers for sale. More exotic items are on display at **True South Trading** at 827 Bank Street, one of a number of Ottawa stores that import jewellery, clothing, and other goods from countries in Central and South America.

Save plenty of time for **Mrs. Tiggy Winkle's/Wizards & Lizards** at 809 Bank Street, because your children won't want to leave. Downstairs, Mrs. Tiggy Winkle's stocks a large and varied selection of toys, gadgets, party favours, and children's music. Upstairs, Wizards & Lizards carries just about anything for the budding science major. Both floors are spacious and exceedingly child-friendly. The staff are usually university-aged and eager to help.

Another popular stop for kids in the Glebe is **Puggwash Children's Books** at 801 Bank Street. Here again, the staff are generally very knowledgeable and friendly. Books of a much different nature can be found at **Octopus Books** at 798 Bank Street. One of Canada's first alternative bookstores (it published an underground newspaper for several years as well), Octopus has broadened its range beyond socialist tracts, but it retains its political bent. It has extensive sections on feminism and alternative medicine, and many books in translation from other countries. It is also an excellent source of information on cultural activities in the city.

Next door, at 798 Bank Street, is **Arbour Recycled Products**, which carries a wide variety of recycled papers, but also more arcane items like hemp clothing. Back on the east side of the street, **Dilemme Gift Shop** at 773 Bank Street is another shop that handles merchandise from Central and South America. Its selection of bright cotton clothing can be compelling if the humidity and heat are making life uncomfortable.

If you're feeling peckish at this point, you have numerous options. Two favourites are **Von's** at 823 Bank Street, a cosy neighbourhood bistro with wonderful Belgian pastries, and **Feleena's** at 742 Bank Street. Tex-Mex food is pretty standard these days, but Feleena's specializes in dishes from central and southern Mexico. The black bean soup is particularly fine. If lunch has aroused your own love of cooking, drop into **The Great Glebe Emporium** at 724 Bank Street. The large store is filled with housewares, including a vast range of kitchen tools and gizmos.

Continue north on Bank to Clemow Avenue. Turn right and enjoy some of the best examples of classic Ottawa architecture from the turn of the century. At O'Connor Street, jog right onto Linden Terrace where it parallels picturesque Central Park. Linden takes you back to the familiar ground of the Queen Elizabeth Driveway.

When it's time to refuel

The knock against Ottawa used to be that there was nowhere to eat, unless you liked roast beef or North American–style Chinese food. All that changed in the 1970s, when restaurants began sprouting on the Byward Market like shitake mushrooms and large numbers of immigrants brought their cultures to the city. Today, Ottawa has many theme restaurants that kids love, as well as an extensive array of ethnic eateries — particularly Lebanese, Vietnamese, and Indian. Tourists are so numerous in central Ottawa that most restaurants are comfortable with children, but we've chosen a number that offer food or features that have stood the test of time.

In addition to these choices, you will find the usual variety of fast-food outlets, as well as many carry-out counters in the basements of the major downtown shopping malls and office towers.

Colonnade Restaurant: There's little on the exterior to indicate that the 200-seat Colonnade is the long-time heavyweight champion of pizza in Ottawa. It sits unobtrusively at the bottom of a nondescript older building and eschews fancy signs or gimmicks. The truth is, the Colonnade doesn't need marketing; the lunch hour brings hordes without any advertising, and people send taxis to pick up their pizzas, because the restaurant does not deliver. Just five short blocks from the Canadian Museum of Nature, the Colonnade is ideally situated for visitors who need calories after a few hours of examining dinosaur bones and rocks. 280 Metcalfe Street, 237-3179.

Druxy's Famous Deli Sandwiches: Ottawa has six locations of this cafeteria-style deli chain, primarily in large commercial office towers. Since they cater to office workers, you can expect brisk service and a wide range of sandwiches, soup, and salads, to either eat in or carryout. The packaging makes Druxy's outlets handy places to stock up for a picnic lunch.

Marchélino by Mövenpick: Located in the lower food court level of the Rideau Centre shopping mall, 569-4934, this branch of the Mövenpick chain has the chaotic variety of a bazaar — enough choice to suit the pickiest eater. Cooked to order while you wait are pasta, seafood, or pizza. Breads and pastries are baked throughout the day to keep everything fresh. Open until 11 pm nightly, this is a terrific place to grab a bite after a movie or an evening at a festival.

The Eager Beaver: Taking a page from the Roots marketing book, this Byward Market restaurant has set out to prove that Canada doesn't have to take a back seat to any other culinary culture. From the rock music on the sound system to the huge papier-mâché reproductions of beavers and bluejays, everything here is Canadian. The adventurous ones in your group might want to try a bison burger, while others may prefer tried-and-true regional favourites like tourtière and side ribs. 77 Clarence Street, 562-1222.

Zak's Diner: The fifties were never this fabulous, but who cares? Revisionist history has its place when it paints everything in bright candy-apple hues, vinyl, and chrome. Archie and Veronica wouldn't seem out of place here ordering shakes, fries, and meatloaf just like Mom used to make. The portions are huge, the atmosphere kinetic, and the food surprisingly good for a restaurant that trades on a theme. 16 Byward Market, 241-2401.

7: Just beyond the fringe

Long-time Ottawans are almost immune to compliments about how green their city is; it's easy to take this proximity to nature for granted. For visitors, though, the rural attractions in the region may be as interesting as the major urban monuments and museums. The best thing is that, with a car, you can tack these side-trips onto your time in Ottawa without passing up any of the city's main sights. With the exception of Parc Oméga, which is about a one-hour drive, all these attractions are within

North

Brébeuf Park

> **Where?** Bégin Street at the Ottawa River, Hull
> **Extras:** Free parking, no washrooms, wheelchair accessible

Named for the 17th-century Jesuit missionary Jean de Brébeuf, who became a martyr when he was mur-dered by Huron Indians, this riverside park is a lovely urban oasis. Adjacent to the Little Chaudière Rapids, the park is built on the site of the Voyageur Portage, the trail used for thousands of years by natives and French traders. A statue of Father Brébeuf was erected in the park in 1926. This is an ideal spot to gain a different perspective on the Ottawa skyline.

Gatineau Park lookout

Gatineau Park ✱

Where? Gatineau Park Visitor Centre, 318 Meech Lake Road, Old Chelsea, Quebec, Exit 12 on Highway 5 north
819-827-2020

When? Mid-May to October 31, daily 9 am–6 pm; November 1 to mid-May, weekdays 9:30 am–4:30 pm, weekends 9 am–5 pm

Extras: Parking $6, outhouses, picnic tables, barbecues, restaurant and general store at Visitor Centre, snackbar and general store at Lac Philippe, cross-country ski trails and huts (ski pass $7 for adults, $4.50 children/seniors), hiking trails, mountain bike trails, lake beaches, fishing. Detailed map of the park available at the Visitor Centre for $3.

This large — 356 square kilometres (140 square miles) — park was formed in the 1930s, when the federal government purchased the land to head off the wholesale harvesting of trees for firewood. The area had been the passion of Prime Minister William Lyon Mackenzie King since he had first visited it by bicycle on Thanksgiving Day, 1900. His estate (see pages 78-79) is one of the park's highlights. Other highlights are the wildlife —

including white-tailed deer, wolves, bears, and beavers — and the many fine lookouts and lakes.

The park offers year-round recreation, ranging from hiking, biking, swimming, and fishing to cross-country skiing and snowshoeing. The 125 kilometres (78 miles) of trails are patrolled by volunteers. Most trails are designated for both hikers and mountain bikers, so be sure to share the road, whatever your means of transportation. Throughout the year, the National Capital Commission runs scheduled events, including a spring festival, ecological events for Earth Day, National Parks Day celebrations, and activities to coincide with the brilliant fall foliage.

The best place to begin any activity is at the Visitor Centre on Meech Lake Road in Old Chelsea.

Leamy Lake Ecological Park ✱

Where? Leamy Lake Parkway, west of the Gatineau River off Fournier Boulevard, Hull
1-800-465-1867

Extras: Parking $5 ($3 for seniors), washrooms and showers, picnic tables, snackbar, hiking trails, lake swimming, windsurfing rentals, fishing

Running along the western shore of the Gatineau River, the Leamy Lake Ecological Park has an abundance of birdlife, as well as excellent aquatic facilities on the lake itself. The park is heavily treed, despite its proximity to the urban parts of Hull and Gatineau.

Hull-Chelsea-Wakefield Railroad ✱

Where? 165 Deveault Street, Hull
819-778-7246
When? Mid-May to Canada Day, Labour Day to late October, Wednesdays, Saturdays, Sundays, and holidays 1:30 pm; Canada Day to Labour Day, daily 1:30 pm
How much? Round-trip fare for adults $23, seniors $21, students over 12 $19.50, children under 13 $11; one-way fare is $19.50 for all ages

The HCW Steam Train at Wakefield

How long? ½ day
Extras: Free parking, washrooms on train and at Hull Station, partially wheelchair and stroller accessible

Older Ottawans fondly remember the days when a ski train ran from Ottawa north along the Gatineau River into the hills. For many years, there was no passenger service into the Gatineaus. Now an enterprising business has brought the train back once again. Old Number 909, a 1907-vintage steam engine, pulls out of the station at 1:30 pm for the 45-minute journey to Wakefield, a picturesque village that has long attracted artists and musicians. Recently the **Black Sheep Inn** at Wakefield's main intersection has become one of the region's most popular music venues. The Sunday matinée concert showcases acoustic music by some of Ottawa's top performers. The two-hour stopover gives you plenty of time to poke around the village's shops, enjoy a late lunch, and watch the river roll lazily by. While pricey, the trip presents a rare opportunity to experience the sounds, smells, and sooty sight of a working steam engine, and the views along the riverside tracks are impressive, especially when the leaves are ablaze with colour.

111

East

Cumberland ✳ Township Museum

Where? 2940 Queen Street (Regional Road 34), Cumberland
833-3059

When? Victoria Day to Thanksgiving, Tuesdays–Fridays 10 am–5 pm, Saturdays and Sundays 11 am–5 pm

How much? Adults $5, seniors and children 5–18 $4, children under 5 free

How long? 1–2 hours

Extras: Free parking, washrooms with diaper-changing facilities, snackbar, partially wheelchair and stroller accessible

You can sample farm life in the 1920s on this 40-hectare (100-acre) homestead. There are more than 20 buildings on the site, including a train station, church, and barn. The museum plays host to a large number of school groups throughout the year, and visiting families are welcome to join the group activities, which include demonstrations of the effect of technology on rural life. Using young amateur

A newborn lamb at the Cumberland Museum

actors, the museum does a good job of bringing history to life and transporting visitors back in time.

Parc Oméga ✳

Where? Route 323, Montebello, Quebec, 3 kilometres (2 miles) north of Highway 148
819-423-5487

When? June 1 to September 30, daily 10 am–7 pm; October 1 to May 30, daily 10 am–4 pm

How much? July and August, adults $9, children 6–15 $4.50, children under 6 free; June, September, and October, adults $8, children 6–15 $4; November through May, adults $6, children $3

How long? 2–3 hours
Extras: Free parking, washrooms, picnic area, snackbar, fully wheelchair and stroller accessible, playground, souvenir stand; binoculars are recommended.
Note: Visitors must stay in their cars in the animal section; pets are not permitted.

Drive-through wild animal parks can be a depressing experience. We remember a horrible one in rural New Jersey where the lions and llamas looked like they were being poisoned by the carbon monoxide fumes, and the heat coming off the pavement was staggering. The 607-hectare (1500-acre) Parc Oméga is nothing like that. The animals — including bison, wapitis, black bears, wild sheep, and boars — are in a natural setting, and the area is large enough that they can wander at will. While you drive through the park, you can tune your car radio to 88.1 FM and hear a running bilingual commentary about the wildlife. During the summer, you can also see a display of birds of prey.

While you're in Montebello, you might also want to visit Manoir Papineau, a national historic site with a gorgeous 19th-century manor house and a theatrical presentation on the turbulent political events of the era. The other main feature of the village is the renowned Château Montebello Hotel, the world's largest log structure and the site of a G-7 world leaders' summit in the 1980s.

Patterson's Berry Farm

Where? 8777 Cooper Hill Road, Edwards, Ontario, Exit 96 on Highway 417 east 821-1230
When? May 1 to October 31, daily 8 am–8 pm; November 1 to April 30, daily 10 am–4 pm
How much? $1–$4, depending on events
How long? 1 hour
Extras: Free parking, washrooms, hot chocolate and cider available in winter, sleigh rides (seasonal)

U-pick berry farms have become a popular summertime destination for Ottawans. Patterson's takes the trend one step further, creating a year-round agricultural attraction with pony rides and 13 varieties of farm animals. In the seasons when the strawberries and raspberries aren't ripe, families can visit the farm's large pumpkin patch, enjoy a sleigh ride, or sample the products of the sugarbush. Kids can test their mettle in the haunted house year-round. Prices at Patterson's vary according to the event.

South

Baxter Conservation Area/Fillmore R. Park Nut Grove ✱

Where? 5 kilometres (3 miles) south of Kars, Ontario, on Dilworth Road 692-3571 or 1-800-267-3504
How much? $5 per vehicle
Extras: Free parking, washrooms, picnic tables, barbecue grills, conservation centre, nature trails, cross-country ski trails, swimming

We'll admit to a certain bias about this destination, since it's only 10 minutes from our door, but we aren't the only ones who appreciate the serenity

you can find here on the banks of the Rideau River. The only sound that disrupts nature here comes from the single-engine planes at the adjacent airstrip, which is also the headquarters for a glider club.

To the left as you enter is a small beach. The beach is unsupervised, but the water is shallow enough at the shore to make it well suited for toddlers. The swimming area is marked by rope. Just off the beach are a number of elevated barbecues, picnic tables, and washrooms.

The **Patrick J. McManus Conservation Centre** is used primarily by school groups on weekdays, but the Rideau Valley Conservation Authority runs weekend interpretation programs several times a year as well (call ahead for times and programs). Several trails begin at the centre, giving you the choice of encircling the thick grove of alder trees, or bisecting it. In the winter, the trails are designated for cross-country skiing or snowshoeing.

The alder grove is bordered by a marsh on its western edge. Crossing the wooden bridge takes you into the **Fillmore R. Park Nut Grove**,

The McManus Centre at the Baxter Conservation Area

named for a charter member of the Ottawa chapter of the Society of Ontario Nut Growers. The park contains 30 varieties of nut- and bean-bearing trees and shrubs, and is the only nut park in eastern Ontario. During duck-hunting season, signs warn you that it's unsafe to cross the marsh. However, you can also reach the nut park from another parking lot further west on Dilworth Road.

Valleyview Little Animal Farm

Where? 4750 Fallowfield Road, west of Moodie Drive, Nepean
591-1126

When? March Break to October 31, weekdays 10 am–3 pm, weekends 10 am–4 pm, closed Mondays except holidays
How much? $3.75
Extras: Free parking, washrooms, indoor and outdoor picnic areas, snackbar, gift shop, partially wheelchair and stroller accessible, playground, special seasonal activities

Younger children will enjoy the casual ambience of this combination petting zoo and heritage farming exhibit. In addition to a small collection of cuddly animals, there's a miniature train kids can ride, a duckpond, and a barn that dates back to the 1890s. Valleyview is at its best in the

115

fall when it's harvest time and the pumpkin patch is full to bursting.

Watson's Mill

Where? 5525 Dickinson Street, Manotick, Ontario, just south of Bridge Street 692-3571 or 1-800-267-3504
When? June to September, Thursdays–Sundays 10 am–5 pm, Mondays–Wednesdays, flexible hours; call ahead
How much? $1 per person
How long? ½ hour
Extras: Free parking, no washrooms

Aside from its annual Fringe Festival (see page 133), Manotick has made its name by preserving history. The showpiece in this heritage movement is the gorgeous stone grist mill that dates from the 1860s. Despite its beauty, the mill has a grisly history. In its early years, the mill's owner brought his new bride to see the place and she fell into the machinery. So there's a ghost, natch, which only adds to the intrigue for kids. Like so many of Ottawa's best heritage attractions, Watson's Mill has not been commercialized;

interpretation experts from the Rideau Valley Conservation Authority conduct tours and run workshops on how the mill works. Little ones in your group will enjoy visiting the many ducks that gather near the small set of falls that powers the mill.

The mill tour doesn't take long, but if you enjoy boutiques and heritage buildings you can easily spend an afternoon in Manotick.

Wild Bird Care Centre ✱

Where? Moodie Drive, south of Knoxdale Road, Nepean 828-2849
When? Daily 11 am–4 pm
How much? Free, but donations are accepted
Extras: Free parking, no washrooms, gift shop

Nepean resident Kathy Nihei's passion for birds has become renowned locally, and her Wild Bird Care Centre has become a sanctuary for injured and ailing birds from many sources. The birds are nursed back to health and released. There is always a wide array of birds on the mend here, which you can view through large windows, and the gift shop has a good selection of items for the birder.

The Wild Bird Care Centre is located in the **Stony Swamp Conservation Area**, a sanctuary for many types of birds and larger animals. The Jack Pine Trail, which starts across Moodie Drive from the centre, offers a pretty walk or ski for 4 kilometres (2.5 miles) through the woods.

West

Pinhey's Point/ Horaceville

Where? On the Ottawa River in the northwest corner of rural Kanata, north of Regional Road 21 between Regional Roads 109 and 129
592-4281
When? Late June to Labour Day, Tuesdays–Sundays 10 am–5 pm
How much? Free, but donations are encouraged for use in reconstruction
Extras: Free parking, washrooms, picnic area

The former home of Upper Canada parliamentarian Hamnett Kirkes Pinhey (1784–1857) has become a

heritage site and waterfront park. The manor house was built in stages between 1820 and 1848, and now is the site of exhibits and interpretive tours by Kanata's Parks and Recreation department.

Stittsville Flea Market

Where? 6176 Hazeldean Road, Stittsville, exit 140 on Highway 417 west
836-5612
When? Sundays 9 am–5 pm
Extras: Parking $1.25, washrooms, snackbar

Eastern Ontario's largest indoor/outdoor market features more than 450 vendors and a staggering range of goods. If you can hang it on a wall, wear it, or collect it, you'll probably find it for sale here. Flea markets aren't everyone's idea of a good time, but if you like shopping in anticipation of finding a terrific bargain or haggling over prices, this can be a great way to spend a few hours on a Sunday. It's also a great place to meet genuine Ottawans at the peak of tourist season, when almost everyone downtown has a camera slung around their neck.

8: Ottawa's assorted sports

Sports of all types are exceptionally popular in the capital region. Joggers, cyclists, and in-line skaters fill the many recreational pathways around the city, the Rideau Canal is covered with skaters from Christmas until March, and skiers flock to the nearby Gatineau Hills on weekends. Minor sports have a long history of success locally, and more recently, professional baseball and hockey have come to town as well. Whatever your family's sports, Ottawa's got your ticket to watch or play.

Because of the large concentration of young families in Ottawa's suburbs, the three large satellite cities all have recreation centres and extensive physical fitness programs. Call each city's recreation department for more information: Gloucester, 748-4100; Kanata, 592-4281; Nepean, 727-6641.

Auto racing

You don't have to be a good ol' boy or a dyed-in-the-wool motorhead to like the roar and excitement of stock-car racing. **Ottawa Valley Speedway** at 1195 Carp Road, 831-1360, 30 minutes west of the city near Stittsville, features several classes of racing throughout the summer.

Baseball

The Triple-A farm club of the Montreal Expos, the **Ottawa Lynx** won the championship of their league in 1995 — their third year in operation. Ottawans fell in love with the

Lynx as soon as they hit town, and one visit to the ball park will show you why. Unlike "the bigs," minor-league ball is played up close and personal. Located just north of the train station beside Highway 417, **Ottawa Stadium** is compact and there isn't a bad seat in the place. The team has a friendly, huggable mascot named Lenny (a lynx, of course), lots of fan giveaways, and a pre-game autograph session with a different player every game. Best of all, the price is right. You can melt your credit card taking your family out to the old ball game in the major leagues, but Lynx tickets start at $4.25 and run up to $8.45 for field-level seats. Game-day tickets are usually available, but call ahead (749-9947 or 1-800-663-0985) to be sure. Even if you're not a diehard baseball fan, it's tough not to have a good time when the Lynx are in town.

Fastball and softball are also very popular in Ottawa and environs. Numerous leagues are active in the spring and summer. You can find a game to watch at any of the local parks that have ball diamonds, or check the listings in the daily newspapers.

Basketball

If you have a young hoops fan, he or she might want to join a

Lenny, mascot of the Ottawa Lynx

pick-up game at the public court in the park at Elgin and Frank Streets. The competition gets pretty fierce in the late afternoon, when many former university varsity players take the court.

Boating

Canoes and pedal-boats can be rented at the **Dow's Lake Pavilion** (232-1001) on the Rideau Canal, and in Quebec at Lac la Pêche and Lac Philippe in **Gatineau Park** (819-827-2020).

Pontoon boats, which can hold up to eight people, are available at the **Hull Marina** (819-595-0909) from May to September.

High-speed Grand Prix powerboat racing comes to the Ottawa River over the Canada Day holiday with the **Gatineau International Regatta** (819-246-7421). The best viewing is from Jacques Cartier Street in Gatineau, across the river from Rockcliffe Park.

The Canadian catamaran championship is the highlight of **Summer Fest** at Aylmer's **Marina Park** (819-782-8678).

Fishing

There is no shortage of rivers and lakes to fish near Ottawa, and some anglers even toss lines into the Rideau River at Hog's Back. Licences are required in both Ontario and Quebec. You can call the appropriate provincial ministries (238-3630 in Ontario, 819-771-4840 in Quebec) for information on purchasing a licence and catch restrictions.

Canoeing at Dow's Lake

Fishing is not permitted in Gatineau Park's Mousseau and Édouard Lakes.

Fitness

The Metro Central branch of the **YM-YWCA of Ottawa-Carleton** at 180 Argyle Street welcomes Y members from Canada or the United States at no charge. Playcare service for the children of members who are using the facilities costs $2. The guest of a member can work out for $5 and get playcare service for $4. Non-members pay $10 and $3. Playcare is available for children 6 months to 7 years and is offered Mondays–Sundays in the morning, Mondays–Thursdays in the evening. Call 788-5000 for information.

Football

The **Ottawa Rough Riders**, Ottawa's entry in the Canadian Football League, have been down so long that it's hard to remember the last winning season, or a season when the team wasn't rife with controversy. In the last decade there have been several owners, numerous financial crises, and so many coaches that no one can remember all their names. Still, the fans have stayed with them, ever hopeful that the team's fortunes will turn around again. On a crisp autumn afternoon, the atmosphere in **Frank Clair Stadium** (Lansdowne Park, Bank Street at the Queen Elizabeth Driveway) — the team's home for almost a century — can make even a cynic a believer. The top price, $38.50, is a little steep, but decent seats on the south side of the stadium can be purchased for $11.50. Call 235-2200.

Game rooms

The introduction of self-contained, secure game rooms is a burgeoning trend in many large cities, and Ottawa is no exception. These indoor playgrounds, all within 20 minutes' drive of downtown, are great places for kids to blow off steam in a safe environment, and provide a welcome break for parents. They are not babysitting services, however. At least one parent must remain at all times, unless stated otherwise.

Cosmic Adventures
1373 Ogilvie Road, Gloucester
742-8989
Billed as "Canada's largest

Bouncing around at Tunnels of Fun

indoor space-age family play-ground," Cosmic Adventures uses outer space as the theme for a four-level series of tunnels, slides, and computer games areas. Free for adults and children under 2, $4.99 for children 2–4, and $7.99 for children over 4. Playtime is unlimited.

GymJam
1642 Merivale Road, Nepean
723-7529
Located in a large mall, which also houses a Y fitness centre, GymJam offers unlimited play-time with tunnels, crafts, and computer games for children up to 12. In addition to this basic service, which costs $4.99 for children under 2 and $6.99 for others, GymJam specializes in birthday parties and secure overnight sleepovers for large groups.

Laser Quest
1800 St. Laurent Boulevard
526-4000
Players over 6 can test their reflexes and agility in a battle with laser guns. Games cost $7 each and last 15 minutes. Weekend afternoons are the best time for younger players. Parents are not required to accompany children.

Tunnels of Fun
19 Stafford Road, Nepean
721-3866
Children 2–12 can explore mazes, work out on the tram-

poline, or have fun with balls. Unlimited use of the main play area is $6.99 per child; no charge for adults. A separate, smaller room is reserved for children under 3, who pay $4.99.

Golf

Four public courses in the area welcome visitors. Barring exceptionally bad or good weather, local courses are usually open by the first week of May and stay open until mid-October. Call the course managers for more information.

Canadian Golf and Country Club
Ashton, Ontario, 45 minutes from downtown
780-3565

Edelweiss Golf and Country Club
Wakefield, Quebec, 20 minutes from downtown
819-459-2331

Manderley on the Green
North Gower, Ontario, 45 minutes from downtown
489-2066

Mont Cascades Golf Club
Cantley, Quebec, 20 minutes from downtown
819-459-2980

Harness racing

The season at **Rideau Carleton Raceway**, 4837 Albion Road in Gloucester, lasts from July 1 to November 30 and includes some important races like the Des Smith Classic. The park has an enclosed grandstand and a restaurant with an excellent view of the track. Call 822-2211 for information.

Hiking

Gatineau Park offers unlimited opportunities for hiking, suited to all fitness levels. There are many picnic and rest areas along the trails. Pick up a trail map at the Gatineau Park Visitor Centre, 318 Meech Lake Road, Old Chelsea, Quebec, exit 12 on Highway 5 north (819-827-2020).

Also on the Quebec side of the river, there is hiking in **Lac Beauchamp Park** on Maloney Boulevard in Gatineau (819-669-2548).

On the Ontario side, the National Capital Commission maintains a number of trails in its **Greenbelt**. Maps are available at Canada's Capital Information Centre, 14 Metcalfe Street.

If you want to go further afield, you can pick up part of the **Rideau Trail**, which runs all the way to Kingston. Call the Rideau Trail Association at 730-2229.

Hockey

The **Ottawa Senators**, the capital's National Hockey League team, haven't been competitive since the franchise was awarded in the early 1990s. But 1996 brought a brand new 18,500-seat stadium, the **Corel Centre**, and the hope that a new home will help turn things around. Built in Kanata, in the rural west end of the capital region, the Corel Centre is a state-of-the-art facility, with a Hard Rock Café and numerous food courts. All that comfort, and NHL action, doesn't come cheap, of course. Tickets start at $24 and escalate to $95. To reach 1000 Palladium Drive, exit south from Highway 417 at Terry Fox Drive and follow the signs. Call 721-4300 or 1-800-444-7367.

The **Ottawa 67s** (232-6767) play Major Junior-A hockey, one level below the NHL, at the Senators' former home, the **Ottawa Civic Centre**, Bank Street at the Queen Elizabeth Driveway. The

The Corel Centre, new home of the NHL Ottawa Senators

season begins in early September and ends in the spring.

Horseback riding

One of the best ways to see Gatineau Park is from horseback. **Captiva Farm** in Wakefield, Quebec (819-459-2769), rents mounts of all sizes for one-hour guided rides on 20 kilometres (12$\frac{1}{2}$ miles) of trails. On the weekends, horses for adults are $22, ponies $15; on weekdays, horses are $17. Children who want to ride must be at least 8.

The **Double-D Ranch** on Highway 17 in Cumberland, 833-2317, offers riding on groomed trails, May to October, for visitors 8 and older. The cost is $15 per hour.

Located in Fitzroy Harbour, west of Ottawa, **Pinto Valley Ranch** (623-3439) rents horses for $15 an hour. Younger children can ride a pony inside a corral for $7.50 per $\frac{1}{2}$ hour.

Ice skating

In addition to skating on the **Rideau Canal** (see pages 66-67), there are many other places, both indoor and outdoor, where you can strap on the blades.

The City of Ottawa offers public skating at 11 arenas and several outdoor rinks. Call 564-1181 for locations and times.

The other cities within the Regional Municipality of Ottawa-Carleton also have indoor arenas with scheduled public skating. The arenas are listed in the Blue Pages of the Ottawa-Hull phone book.

In Hull, there is outdoor skating on **Brewery Creek**; call 819-595-7175.

In Gatineau, skating is available on **Lac Beauchamp**; call 819-669-2548.

In-line skating

In-line skating is, strictly speaking, illegal on city streets and sidewalks, but the by-law has not been enforced and there is no shortage of skaters. Skating is permitted on the bicycle paths, provided you share the right of way with others. Skates can be rented at **Rent-a-Bike** behind the Château Laurier Hotel (see page 88). The city offers lessons; call 564-1094.

Marathons

The city's many parkways and nature paths encourage activity, so it's not surprising that the area has more than its share of marathon runners and triathletes. The **Colonel By Triathlon** (737-3448) is staged each June at the Rideau Canoe Club at Mooney's Bay, Riverside Drive at Ridgewood Avenue. The events include canoe, bicycle, and foot races. The **National Capital Triathlon** takes place at the same location in mid-July (737-3448).

For marathoners, the highlight of the year comes on Victoria Day weekend with the **National Capital Race Weekend** (234-2221). The race begins and ends at Carleton University, Bronson Avenue at Sunnyside Avenue.

Skiing and snowboarding

Cross-country

The most extensive cross-country trails are in Gatineau Park (see pages 109-10), but there are also some in the NCC's **Greenbelt**. Maps are available at Canada's Capital Information Centre, 14 Metcalfe Street. The City of Ottawa operates a 2-kilometre (1.25-mile) circuit at the **Terry Fox Athletic Facility**,

Riverside Drive at Ridgewood Avenue (564-1094).

In Quebec, trails are maintained at **Lac Beauchamp Park** in Gatineau (819-669-2548) and **Lac des Fées** in Hull (819-595-7405).

No matter what your skill level, there's a class for you in the 170-kilometre (106-mile) **Canadian Ski Marathon**, which is held every February between Lachute and Hull, with an overnight stop at Montebello, Quebec. Call 819-663-7383 for information.

If you prefer to watch, the **Keskinada Loppet** brings some of the world's best to Gatineau Park in mid-February. Call 819-827-4641.

Downhill

Few major cities have such close proximity to ski areas. The elevation of the Gatineau Hills is not as high as the Laurentians or the Adirondacks several hours away, but the facilities are extensive. All the ski areas have hills set aside for snowboarders as well. For regularly updated ski reports, call 762-5414. There are four areas within a 30-minute drive of downtown. Lift rates vary widely, but

Cooling off at Mooney's Bay Beach

average $10 for half-days and $20 for full days.

Edelweiss Valley Ski Resort

Wakefield, Quebec
819-459-2328
Eighteen slopes with four lifts, 200-metre (656-foot) vertical drop, day and night skiing.

Mount Cascades

Cantley, Quebec
819-827-0301
Twelve slopes with five lifts, 160-metre (525-foot) vertical drop, day and night skiing.

Ski Fortune

Old Chelsea, Quebec
819-827-1717
Fourteen slopes with four lifts,

228-metre (748-foot) vertical drop, day and night skiing.

Vorlage Ski and Recreation Area

Wakefield, Quebec
819-459-2302
Fifteen slopes with six lifts, 150-metre (492-foot) vertical drop, day and night skiing.

Swimming, waterslides, wave pools

Beaches

The City of Ottawa operates three free public beaches: **Britannia Bay**, Britannia Road at the Ottawa River; **Mooney's Bay** (Rideau River), Riverside Drive at Ridgewood

Avenue; and **Westboro Beach**, Ottawa River Parkway west of Island Park Drive. Lifeguards are on duty mid-June to Labour Day, 11 am–7 pm. The water quality is checked regularly, and the beaches are sometimes forced to close after a heavy rainfall. Call 244-5678 for beach conditions.

South of Ottawa in Rideau Township, there is a pleasant sandy beach on the Rideau River at the **Baxter Conservation Area** (see pages 114-15).

In Quebec, a number of lake and riverside beaches can be found within a 30-minute drive of the city. You'll be charged a user fee, usually about $5 per vehicle, that includes parking.

Aylmer Marina
Highway 148, Aylmer
819-684-5372

Lac la Pêche
Eardley Road off Highway 366 west, Gatineau Park
819-827-2020

Lac Philippe (Breton and Parent Beaches)
Lac Philippe Parkway off Highway 366 west,

Gatineau Park
819-827-2020

Leamy Lake
Leamy Lake Road, Hull
239-5617

Meech Lake (O'Brien and Blanchet Beaches)
Exit 12 off Highway 5 north, Gatineau Park
819-827-2020

Pools
Ottawa, Hull, and the other cities in the region all operate numerous municipal pools. Rates are in the $3–$5 range. The closest indoor pools to central Ottawa are the **Champagne Pool**, 321 King Edward Avenue, 564-1033, the **Jack Purcell Centre**, 320 Jack Purcell Lane at Elgin Street, 564-1027, and the **Plant Bath**, 130 Preston Street, 564-1040. Call 244-5678 in Ottawa, 819-595-7400 in Hull for more information.

Both local universities have scheduled public swims at their large indoor pools. Rates are about $2.50. For **Carleton University**, call 520-5631; for the **University of Ottawa**, 562-5789.

Waterslides

Walter Baker Sports Centre

100 Malvern Drive, Nepean
825-2468

Families $10.45, adults $3.55,
seniors $1.90, children 13–17
$2.75, ages 2–12 $2.25,
under 2 free.

Wavepools

Kanata Leisure Centre

70 Aird Place, Kanata
591-9283

Adults $5.75, children 2–17
$4.25; children under 9 must
be supervised.

Splash

2040 Ogilvie Road, Gloucester
748-4222

Adults $5.35, children 1–18
$3.80; children under 7 require
supervision.

Tennis

The City of Ottawa maintains
a number of public courts.
Lessons can be arranged.
Call 564-1099 for information.

Windsurfing

Windsurfing boards and
lessons are available at two
Ottawa beaches, **Mooney's
Bay** and **Britannia Bay**;
call 244-5300 for information
on either. In Aylmer, Quebec,
lessons and rentals are
available at the **municipal
marina** (819-685-5007);
in Hull, you can find the same
services at **Leamy Lake**
(239-5617).

9: The year in special events

O ttawa's emphasis on tourism has nurtured the growth of a variety of festivals and special events. Some, like Winterlude and Canada Day, draw large crowds, including many people from out of town, while others are smaller, homegrown affairs. All have children's components and allow your family to sample the region's culture at first hand.

The following listings are based on the most recent information available at publication. If you want to plan your time in Ottawa to coincide with one of these events, call the number given to confirm the scheduling of the event and any other details that are important to you.

The dollar signs **($$)** denote paid admission; **FREE** events are noted.

January

Early January: **Governor General's Levée FREE**
Rideau Hall
993-9530
In keeping with tradition, the Governor General ushers in the new year by opening the doors of Rideau Hall to the public. Refreshments are served, and visitors are welcome to look around the public parts of the official residence.

February

First three weekends:
Winterlude FREE
Various locations in Ottawa, Hull, and Gatineau, Quebec
1-800-465-1867 or 239-5000

You can hide from winter, or you can make the most of it. Each February, Ottawans take to the frozen Rideau Canal and the snowy parks to celebrate in what has become North America's largest winter carnival. Regular features include a snow sculpture contest on Dow's Lake, an outdoor pop music concert, and figure skating performances on the canal at Fifth Avenue.

In Hull's Jacques Cartier Park, tonnes of snow are turned into slides, tunnels, and castles for children to enjoy.

***Mid-month:* Aylmer Winter Carnival FREE**
Various locations in Aylmer, Quebec, 15 minutes by car from Ottawa
819-684-5372

Winter celebrations in this west Quebec bedroom community tend to be more low-key and closer to the grass-roots than Winterlude. Events include dogsled, snowmobile, and car races, winter sports, and a barn dance.

April

***Two weeks at month's end:*
Ottawa Valley Book Festival
FREE and $$**
National Library of Canada and other locations
241-4031

A high-profile gala featuring nationally known authors and the annual literary awards are the highlights of this festival, founded in 1985. Several events are geared to younger readers, including storytelling sessions and readings by children's authors. Tickets for the gala should be purchased in advance.

An ice hog and friend at Winterlude

The Tulip Festival is a May highlight

May

Victoria Day weekend:
Canadian Tulip Festival
FREE and $$
Major's Hill Park and other
locations
567-4447

It started with a gift of tulip
bulbs from Holland as thanks
for harbouring the Dutch royal
family during World War II.
Today, more than 3 million
tulips form a multicoloured
backdrop to a 6-day celebra-
tion of spring. Events include
concerts, fireworks, and a craft
fair. The highest-profile ele-
ment is the Rideau Canal
Flotilla. Hundreds of boaters
dress up their craft with deco-
rations and set off slowly down
the canal. The best places to
watch the flotilla are the path-
ways that run parallel to the
canal from Dow's Lake to the
National Arts Centre.

June

First week: **Children's**
Festival $$
Canadian Museum of Nature
728-5863

The long-running Children's
Festival stages events
throughout the year but focus-
es its efforts each June on five
days of mime, dance, theatre,

and music aimed primarily at kids under 12. Performers include local favourites, as well as well-known national and international acts like Eric Nagler. Events are held on the lawn outside the historic Victoria Memorial Museum Building, site of the Canadian Museum of Nature, so combining festival acts with a visit to the dinos inside is a natural. Some events sell out quickly, so it's a good idea to purchase tickets as soon as possible.

Mid-month: Manotick Fringe Festival $$
Various locations in Manotick, 30 minutes by car from Ottawa
692-0548

It would be difficult to find a more unlikely setting for a festival of alternative theatre than the wealthy town of Manotick. Nevertheless, this historic community on the banks of the Rideau provides some interesting settings, including an old firehall. Like any of the fringe festivals that have sprung up across Canada, the Manotick Fringe includes many performances not intended for young audiences, but the festival tries to include family events in its schedule as well.

Third weekend: Le Franco $$
Various locations, including Confederation Park on Elgin Street
741-9399

Originally a festival to celebrate the unique heritage of Franco-Ontarians, the festival has changed its focus and now bills itself as the largest celebration of francophone culture in North America. Some residents of New Orleans might dispute that claim, but Le Franco shows that some Ottawans truly know how to "laisser les bons temps rouler." Entertainment includes street performers and concerts, and there are samples of various forms of French cooking.

Last weekend: National Capital Air Show $$
Macdonald-Cartier International Airport
526-1030

Operating on a smaller scale than the major European air shows, this makes for an interesting afternoon, especially if you have plane buffs in your group. There are vintage planes on display and acrobatic planes in the air. For those who like their fun on the ground, there's also a small midway.

July

***July 1:* Canada Day FREE**
Parliament Hill and various
other sites
239-5000

Is Ottawa staid? You wouldn't
think so on Canada Day. From
morning until after midnight,
the streets are filled with people, and Canadian flags flutter
everywhere. Festivities vary
year to year but usually
include many events to celebrate Canada's multicultural
heritage. The day always cul-
minates on Parliament Hill
with a gala concert that is
broadcast on national TV and
a spectacular fireworks display. Our one experience on
the Hill several years ago con-
vinced us that the evening
show is no place for children
under 10; the crowd is just too
large for comfort. The higher
floors of several of the downtown hotels offer far better
viewing of the fireworks, as do
sites along the Quebec side of
the Ottawa River. Wherever
you choose to go to watch,
don't take a car; the traffic jam
after the fireworks can strand
you for hours.

Mid-month for 10 days:
**Ottawa International Jazz
Festival FREE and $$**
Confederation Park on Elgin
Street and various other sites
1-800-267-5288 or 594-3580

Unlike jazz festivals in many
other cities, the Ottawa
International Jazz Festival
keeps its focus on Canadian
artists, limiting the foreign tal-
ent to lesser-known musicians
and keeping admission fees
very low. A $25-per-person
passport provides admission
to about 50 different concerts.
Nightly outdoor shows draw
many families, who sit on lawn
chairs or sprawl on blankets.
Free noontime shows are
held throughout the down-
town area and a few satellite
sites. The festival usually
includes several special
events intended to introduce
young children to jazz.

August

***Weekends:* Cultures
Canada $$**
Various locations, including
the Astrolabe Theatre, the
National Gallery of Canada,
and the Canadian Museum of
Civilization
1-800-465-1867 or 239-5000

Celebrating the country's
diverse cultural make-up,
Cultures Canada concerts

The Central Canada Exhibition draws fun-seekers every August

feature everything from Inuit singers to Celtic folk groups. In addition to low-cost concerts by Canadian artists, the National Gallery of Canada and the Canadian Museum of Civilization also host shows by well-known musicians from various parts of the world. Tickets for the popular international musicians tend to go quickly.

***First weekend:* CKCU International Busker Festival $$**
Sparks Street Mall
788-3573

Ottawa is home to a large number of street performers, and the annual busker festival adds many more from across North America, as well as a few from Europe. Performers include jugglers, fire-eaters, magicians, comedians, and mimes.

***Mid-month for 10 days:* Central Canada Exhibition $$**
Lansdowne Park
237-7222

The "Ex" has its roots in the agricultural fairs of the 1800s, but today it varies little from most other exhibitions and state fairs across the continent. Loud, brash, and expensive, it continues to be a yearly draw

Face painting on Canada Day

for kids, who love the cotton candy, carnival games, and midway rides. Attendance figures have fallen in recent times, causing organizers to shift the emphasis away from the major-name rock concerts that were the staple of the Ex for years to more traditional exhibition fare. For younger children, there are a variety of tamer rides, animal displays, and a petting zoo.

Last weekend: CKCU Ottawa Valley Folk Festival $$
Victoria Island, west of the National Library
788-2898
Although it started only in 1995,

the folk festival dates back to an earlier event, which was sponsored by the same campus radio station. The festival brings in talent from outside Ottawa, but its backbone is the rich contingent of folk musicians who come from this area, including performers like Bruce Cockburn, Colleen Peterson, Valdy, and Lynn Miles. In addition to formal concerts, the festival includes workshops where you can interact with musicians and learn the craft of singing and songwriting.

Gatineau Hot Air Balloon Festival

September

Labour Day weekend:
**Gatineau Hot Air Balloon
Festival $$**
La Baie Park, Gatineau,
Quebec, 15 minutes by car
from Ottawa
1-800-668-8383, 819-243-2330
The sight of a hot air balloon
aloft is always a thrill, so
imagine the sight of 150 of
them. Pilots from around the
world bring crafts in a range
of sizes, shapes, and colours.
In addition to the balloons,
there are more than 200
musical performances and
a midway with 20 rides.

October

Mid-month: **Capital
Agrifest $$**
Lansdowne Park
237-7222
Ottawa's rural roots are
never far beneath the surface.
The Capital Agrifest is a
showcase for farmers from
throughout eastern Ontario
and western Quebec. In
addition to livestock com-
petitions and horse shows,
the festival features step-
dancing and fiddling
demonstrations, a country
crafts display, and a
children's program.

137

November

November 11: **Remembrance Day FREE**
National War Memorial,
Confederation Square
239-5000

Their numbers continue to shrink, but Canada's war veterans still make the pilgrimage to the National War Memorial to remember their fallen comrades. Organized by the Royal Canadian Legion, the national Remembrance Day ceremony draws a large crowd, including many of the Armed Forces personnel who are stationed at National Defence Headquarters. In attendance to place wreaths of poppies at the base of the War Memorial are the Governor General, the Prime Minister, and representatives from many foreign embassies. Young people play a large part in the ceremony, including the Central Choir of the Ottawa Board of Education and youth representatives chosen from across Canada by the Legion. Following the solemn ceremony, the Governor General takes a salute from veterans and members of the Armed Forces as they parade down Wellington Street behind the War Memorial.

December

Beginning the first Thursday, for 10 days: **Ottawa Christmas Craft Sale $$**
Lansdowne Park
241-5777

Founded in 1974, this is one of the oldest and largest craft sales of its kind in North America. The work of 250 artisans from across the country is showcased, including wooden toys, puppets, and children's clothing.

Throughout the month: **Christmas Lights Across Canada FREE**
Parliament Hill and
Confederation Boulevard
239-5000

Early in December, a switch is thrown and the core of Ottawa comes alive with thousands of coloured lights. The official "ceremonial route" that includes parts of Elgin Street, Wellington Street, Rideau Street, and Sussex Drive twinkles all month. The colours are carefully coordinated by the National Capital Commission and guaranteed to chase Scrooge out of town for the holidays.

10: Accommodations: from spartan to spectacular

Like any city that thrives on the tourist trade, the National Capital Region has a wide array of hotels, motels, guest-houses, and campsites. You can choose to pay a premium and stay in a room with a view of history, or park your family a little out of the main-stream. The accommodations we've chosen to highlight all meet the criteria of safe locations, professional staff, and solid track records for service. Those marked with ★ offer outstanding service for families.

All the information here was correct at the end of 1995, but as always it's best to call ahead before you solidify your plans. Ottawa fills with tourists during Winterlude and the Tulip Festival and for several days on either side of Canada Day, so it's advisable to book well in advance if you are planning a visit during those times. In fact, it's always best to book ahead to avoid disappointment.

If you do arrive in town without a reservation, how-ever, the Ottawa Tourism and Convention Authority offers a free last-minute booking service at its National Arts Centre office (see pages 10-11). You can also call ahead to have them locate accommodations (1-800-465-1867). A listing of Ottawa-area accommodations is available on the Internet at *http://www.iatech.com/tour/ hotels/hotq.htm*.

Bed and breakfast homes

Ottawa has a relatively large number of bed and breakfast establishments, many of which are in older homes in the city's historic central neighbourhoods. Your experience at any B&B will depend a great deal on your interaction with your hosts. If you are gregarious, your stay at a B&B could well be the highlight of your vacation. Some innkeepers are willing to share their knowledge of the the city with you, which sometimes includes insights that would otherwise be unavailable. Not all B&Bs welcome children, and we have attempted to determine which ones are suitable for families, with some restrictions, as noted. One of the charms of B&Bs is their individuality, but their diversity results in a wide variation in features and rates. Innkeepers are quite happy to describe their rooms and their distinctive features in loving detail. For additional information about B&Bs in Ottawa, you can also contact:

- **Ottawa Bed and Breakfast**
  488 Cooper Street
  Ottawa ON K1R 5H9
  Tel 563-0161 or
  1-800-461-7889

Ambiance Bed and Breakfast

330 Nepean Street
Ottawa ON K1R 5G6
Tel 563-0421

- 5-minute walk to Parliament Hill
- No age restrictions
- 4 rooms $49–$71; some rooms with private bath; full, healthy breakfast
- Major credit cards
- Free parking
- Air-conditioning; non-smoking
- No TV
- Victorian house

Auberge des Arts ✼

104 Guigues Avenue
Ottawa ON K1N 5H7
Tel 562-0909
Fax 562-0940

- At northern end of Byward Market, 10 minutes from Parliament Hill
- Prefers children over 7
- 3 rooms $55; 1 suite with kitchenette $70; $5–$10 for children; private bath;

full breakfast
- Major credit cards
- Free parking
- Guests may use kitchen
- Air-conditioning; non-smoking
- Cable TV and VCR in suite only

L'Auberge du Marché

87 Guigues Avenue
Ottawa ON K1N 5H8
Tel 241-6610 or 1-800-465-0079

- At northern end of Byward Market, 10 minutes from Parliament Hill
- Prefers children over 7
- 4 rooms $49–$59; 1 suite with private bathroom and kitchen $75; $10 for children ages 7–12, $20 for children over 12; full breakfast
- Visa and Mastercard
- Limited free parking; near-by parking lot $5 per day
- Air-conditioning; non-smoking
- TV in suite only

Beatrice Lyon Guest House 🧸

479 Slater Street
Ottawa ON K1R 5C2
Tel 236-3904

- At western edge of down-town, 5-minute walk from

Parliament Hill
- No age restrictions
- 3 rooms $45; children under 6 free, $5 for children 6–11, $10 ages 12–15, $15 over 15; some private bathrooms; full breakfast
- No credit cards
- Free parking
- Some in-room air-conditioning; no smoking in guest rooms
- TV in rooms

Gasthaus Switzerland Inn

89 Daly Avenue
Ottawa ON K1N 6E6
Tel 237-0335 or 1-800-267-8788
Fax 594-3327

- Near the University of Ottawa, 10-minute walk from Parliament Hill
- Children over 12 only
- 23 rooms $68–$78; $20 for extra persons; private bathrooms; full breakfast
- Major credit cards
- Limited free parking
- Air-conditioning; non-smoking
- Cable TV in rooms
- Swiss-style inn with beautiful garden

141

Le Gîte Park Avenue Bed and Breakfast ✱

54 Park Avenue
Ottawa ON K2P 1B2
Tel 230-9131

- Close to Rideau Canal and Canadian Museum of Nature, 15-minute walk from Parliament Hill
- No age restrictions
- 3 rooms $65; children under 5 free, $10 ages 5–13, $20 over 13; private bath available; full breakfast
- Visa and Mastercard
- Limited free parking
- Guests can use kitchen for making sandwiches
- Air-conditioning; non-smoking
- TV and VCR in common area
- Deck area suitable for children

Haydon House

18 The Driveway
Ottawa ON K2P 1C6
Tel 230-2697

- 10-minute walk from Parliament Hill
- No age restrictions
- 3 rooms $70; children $15; 1 private bath-room; continental breakfast
- No credit cards
- Free parking
- Air-conditioning; no smoking in guest rooms
- TV in common area
- Beautifully renovated old house located steps from Rideau Canal

Olde Bytown Bed and Breakfast

459 Laurier Avenue East
Ottawa ON K1N 6R4
Tel 565-7939
Fax 565-7981

- Near Rideau River and Strathcona Park, 20-minute walk from Parliament Hill
- No age restrictions
- 7 rooms $55–$65; children under 7 free, $10 ages 7–12, $20 over 12; some rooms have private bathrooms; full English or low-calorie breakfast, as well as afternoon tea with scones
- Visa and Mastercard
- Free parking
- Air-conditioning; non-smoking
- TV and VCR in common area

Rideau View Inn

177 Frank Street
Ottawa ON K2P 0X4
Tel 236-9309 Fax 237-6842

- Close to Rideau Canal,
  15-minute walk from
  Parliament Hill
- No age restrictions
- 7 rooms $65–$85; children
  under 5 free, $10 ages
  5 and over; some rooms
  have private bathrooms;
  full breakfast
- Visa card
- Limited free parking
- Air-conditioning;
  non-smoking
- TV and VCR in common
  area
- Victorian house

Campgrounds

One of the advantages of a
smaller city is the proximity
to rural areas. Ottawa has
several campgrounds that
are just a short drive from
downtown, and one that is
right downtown itself.

Camp Hither Hills

5227 Bank Street, Gloucester
(Highway 31)
Tel 822-0509 Fax 822-6413

- 30-minute drive south of
  downtown

- 150 sites, serviced, $13
- Water hookups, showers,
  toilets and dumping station
- Laundry facilities, on-site
  store
- Children's playground, pool

Cantley Camping

100 Ste-Elisabeth, Cantley,
Quebec
Tel 819-827-1056

- 30-minute drive northeast of
  downtown
- 299 sites, serviced, $14.40
  and up
- Water hookups, showers,
  toilets and dumping station
- Laundry facilities, on-site
  store
- Children's playground,
  pool, activity program,
  indoor recreation, fishing

LeBreton Camping

Fleet Street at Booth Street,
Ottawa
Tel 239-5565; June–September
943-0467

- Operated by the National
  Capital Commission
- On historic LeBreton Flats,
  a 10-minute walk from
  Parliament Hill
- 200 sites, not serviced,
  $7.50 per person
- Showers and toilets only

Ottawa-Nepean Municipal Campsite

41 Corkstown Road, Nepean

Tel 828-6632 Fax 727-6613

- Near the National Capital Equestrian Park, a 20-minute drive west of downtown
- 153 sites, serviced, $12 and up
- Water hookups, showers, toilets and dumping station
- Laundry facilities, on-site store
- Children's playground, activity program

Ottawa River Shore Camping

Highway 17, 5 kilometres east of Cumberland

Tel 833-2663

- 45-minute drive east of downtown
- 49 sites, serviced, $14 per person
- Water hookups, showers, toilets and dumping station
- Laundry facilities, on-site store
- Children's playground, pool

Poplar Grove Trailer Park

1554 Highway 31, Gloucester

Tel 821-2973

- 45-minute drive south of downtown
- 250 sites, serviced, $14 and up
- Water hookups, showers, toilets and dumping station
- Laundry facilities, on-site store
- Children's playground, pool, indoor recreation

Recreationland

1566 Canaan Road, Cumberland

Tel 833-2974

Fax 833-1219

- 45-minute drive east of downtown
- 100 sites, serviced, $14 and up
- Water hookups, showers, toilets and dumping station
- Laundry facilities, on-site store
- Children's playground, pool

Hotels

There is nothing quite like a hotel at the end of a hectic day of travel, or after you've walked your feet off sightseeing. An hour in a pool can do wonders to soothe the "travel nerves" that have built up from too much family togetherness, and room service can be a lifesaver when your kids are too tired to cope with one more restaurant meal. Many hotels have changed their attitude towards children over the years, and now treat them with as much respect as their parents. Some even afford them special privileges and treatment. And some in the highest service categories realize that parents appreciate a little time away from their charges. The establishments that go that extra mile are the ones we return to time after time.

Hotel rates vary throughout the year, depending on availability, competition, and special promotional packages. Depending on how you book your room, you may also be able to realize additional discounts. Most hotels offer weekend specials, and some have special family rates. Always ask what's available, and be persistent. Since rates can be affected by so many factors, we have listed the upper price range of each hotel based on the so-called "rack" rate (the price usually posted on the inside of the door) for a room with two large beds:

$	below $100
$$	$100–$125
$$$	$125–$150
$$$$	above $150

Not all rooms in the hotel are guaranteed to have all the features listed here. Check with the hotel to ensure that the room you book has the features you want. Some items such as cots must be reserved in advance. Similarly, check the opening hours of facilities such as swimming pools and laundry rooms.

For those travelling by car, or who plan to rent a car, we have included a number of hotels and motor hotels that are outside the downtown area but on main routes into Ottawa, or close to family attractions.

Downtown hotels

Château Laurier ✱

$$$$
1 Rideau Street
Ottawa ON K1N 9H4
Tel 241-1414 or 1-800-441-1414
Fax 562-7030
When Disney wanted a symbol

The Château Laurier

of Canada for its Epcot Centre in Florida, it chose the turrets and green roof of Ottawa's most distinctive hotel. Built in 1912 as part of the Grand Trunk Pacific Railway system — and connected by tunnel to the old Union Station across the street — the Château was the pet project of hotelier Charles Hays. Hays died when the *Titanic* sank, but the hotel has lived up to his dreams for it. Overlooking the Rideau Canal, the Parliament Buildings, and the Byward Market, the Château is at the city's epicentre. Kids are treated like royalty at the castle, from special check-in kits to a series of programs that run throughout the year. The hotel's Easter egg painting contest, parade, and Mad Hatter Tea are spring highlights. Throughout the summer, the Castle Playroom is open daily, with crafts and movies. In December, children are invited to bring their favourite teddy to the Teddy Bear Tea. The hotel has special seasonal rates.

- 425 rooms
- CAA discount; children

under 18 free

- Parking garage; $12 per day; in-and-out privileges
- Minifridges, coffeemakers in all rooms
- Cable TV; no VCR; pay TV
- Hairdryers
- Cribs free; no cots
- Babysitting available; supervised children's play-room for children over 2, hours vary
- Disabled access
- Non-smoking floors
- No pets
- No laundry facilities; dry cleaning service
- 2 restaurants; children's menu in Wilfrid's
- Indoor pool, sauna, exercise centre; children under 10 must be supervised

Citadel Ottawa Hotel and Convention Centre ✱ $$

101 Lyon Street
Ottawa ON K1R 5T9
Tel 237-3600 or 1-800-567-3600
Fax 237-2351

One of the first buildings to break the longstanding height barrier in downtown Ottawa, the Citadel sits atop an underground shopping mall, just a few blocks from Parliament Hill. Younger kids receive special kits when they check in.

- 394 rooms; 17 suites
- CAA discount; children under 18 free
- Indoor parking; $11 per day; in-and-out privileges
- Minifridges in 51 rooms; minifridges and coffeemakers in 5 suites
- Cable TV; no VCR; pay TV
- Hairdryers in 5 suites
- Cribs and cots free; high chairs, diapers available
- Babysitting available
- Disabled access
- Non-smoking floors
- Pets permitted, with restrictions
- Valet laundry service
- 1 restaurant; children's menu; free continental breakfast served daily
- Indoor pool, health club; children under 12 must be supervised

Days Inn Ottawa City Centre $$$

123 Metcalfe Street
Ottawa ON K1P 5L9
Tel 237-9300 or 1-800-329-7466
Fax 237-2163

Close to Parliament Hill, the

Days Inn has a Frequent Stay Club that offers additional discounts for travellers who visit Ottawa often.

- 144 rooms
- CAA discount; children under 12 free
- Valet underground parking; $10 per day; in-and-out privileges
- Minifridges; microwaves; coffeemakers
- Cable TV; VCR rental; pay TV
- Hairdryers
- Cribs $2; cots $10
- Babysitting available
- Limited disabled access
- Non-smoking floors
- No pets
- No laundry facilities; dry cleaning service
- 1 restaurant; children's menu

Delta Ottawa Hotel and Suites ✱ $$

361 Queen Street
Ottawa ON K1R 7S9
Tel 238-6000 or 1-800-268-1133
Fax 238-2290

Situated at the western edge of the city's core, the Delta is one of several downtown hotels that opened in the late 1970s just blocks from the Supreme Court of Canada and Parliament Hill. Despite its central location, the hotel has kept recreation a priority, and kids love its 2-storey waterslide. Like other Delta properties, the Delta Ottawa has a supervised Children's Creative Centre.

- 271 rooms; 58 suites
- CAA discount; children under 18 free
- Indoor parking; $7–$10 per day, free to CAA members; in-and-out privileges
- Minifridges and coffeemakers in rooms; kitchens and coffeemakers in suites
- Cable TV; no VCR; pay TV
- Hairdryers
- Cribs and cots free
- Babysitting available
- Disabled access
- Non-smoking floors
- Pets permitted
- Coin-op laundry; overnight dry cleaning
- 2 restaurants; 1 has a children's menu; children under 7 eat free
- Indoor pool with waterslide, supervised on weekends, admission restricted weekdays; sauna, whirlpool, health club, video arcade

Howard Johnson Plaza Hotel Ottawa ✸ $

140 Slater Street
Ottawa ON K1P 5H6
Tel 238-2888 or 1-800-446-4656
Fax 235-8421

Like most HoJo's, this one provides a special activity package for younger kids at check-in. The hotel occasionally has promotional gifts available for children. An older hotel that has been renovated several times over the decades, the Howard Johnson Plaza is 4 blocks from Parliament Hill and 2 from the Rideau Canal.

- 107 rooms
- CAA discount; children under 10 free
- Outdoor parking; $10.75 per day; in-and-out privileges
- No kitchen facilities; coffeemakers
- Cable TV; no VCR; pay TV; free Sega Game Gear
- Hairdryers; Jacuzzis on executive floor
- Cribs free; cots $10
- No babysitting available
- No disabled access
- Non-smoking floors
- Pets permitted, with restrictions
- No laundry facilities
- 1 restaurant; children under 10 eat free from children's menu

Lord Elgin Hotel $$$

100 Elgin Street
Ottawa ON K1P 5K8
Tel 235-3333 or 1-800-267-4298
Fax 235-3223

Close to the National War Memorial and Parliament Hill.

- 11 rooms; 300 suites
- CAA discount; children under 19 free
- Underground valet parking; $10 per night; in-and-out privileges
- No kitchen facilities in rooms; minifridges in suites
- Cable TV; no VCR; pay TV
- Hairdryers
- Cribs and cots free
- Babysitting services available
- Disabled access
- Non-smoking floors
- Pets permitted
- No laundry facilities
- 1 restaurant; children's portions available
- Fitness room; children 14 and under admitted under supervision

149

The Lord Elgin Hotel

Novotel Hotel ✸ $$$

33 Nicholas Street
Ottawa ON K1N 9M7
Tel 230-3033 or 1-800-668-6835
Fax 230-7865

Located at the southern end of the Byward Market, a 10-minute walk from Parliament Hill, the Novotel is one of the city's newest hotels. Children are welcomed by the hotel mascot, Dolphi, and presented with free toys and games.

- 282 rooms; 1 suite
- Indoor parking; $12 per night; in-and-out privileges
- Minifridges in 250 units, including suite; some coffeemakers
- Cable TV; no VCR; pay TV
- Hairdryers
- Cribs, cots, and high chairs free
- No babysitting available
- Disabled access
- Non-smoking rooms
- No pets permitted
- No laundry facilities
- 2 restaurants; children's menu; free breakfast for children under 12 with parents
- Pool, fitness room

Quality Hotel by Journey's End $$

290 Rideau Street
Ottawa ON K1N 5Y3
Tel 789-7511 or 1-800-228-5151
Fax 789-2434

At the southeastern edge of the Byward Market, this hotel is 15 minutes from Parliament Hill. It has some seasonal promotional packages geared towards children.

- 212 rooms
- CAA discount; children under 17 free
- Indoor parking $7.50 a night; in-and-out privileges
- No kitchen facilities or coffeemakers
- Cable TV; no VCR; pay TV
- Hairdryers
- Cribs free; cots $4
- Babysitting available
- Disabled access, including 2 fully equipped rooms
- Non-smoking floors
- Pets permitted
- No laundry facilities
- 1 restaurant; children's portions available

Radisson Hotel Ottawa Centre $$$

100 Kent Street
Ottawa ON K1P 5R7
Tel 238-1122 or 1-800-333-3333
Fax 783-4229

The Radisson, close to Parliament Hill, offers occasional packages in conjunction with area museums. One of its dining rooms is a revolving rooftop restaurant; the other is a family-style café with colouring placemats.

- 478 rooms
- CAA discount; children under 19 free
- Nearby parking; $7 a night
- Minifridges; coffeemakers in 30 rooms
- Cable TV; no VCR; pay TV
- Hairdryers
- Cribs, cots, and high chairs free
- Babysitting available
- Disabled access
- Non-smoking floors
- Small pets permitted
- Valet laundry service
- 2 restaurants, 1 with children's menu
- Indoor pool, sauna, whirlpool; small children must be accompanied by an adult

Sheraton Ottawa Hotel and Towers $$$

150 Albert Street
Ottawa ON K1P 5G2
Tel 238-1500 or 1-800-489-8333

The Westin Hotel

Fax 235-2723

Close to Parliament Hill.

- 230 rooms; 6 suites
- CAA discount; children under 17 free
- Underground parking; $15 per night; in-and-out privileges
- Minifridges in 66 rooms, 2 suites; coffeemakers in suites
- Cable TV, no VCR; in-house movies55
- Hairdryers in suites
- Cribs, cots, high chairs, and booster seats free
- Babysitting available
- Disabled access
- Non-smoking floors
- Pets permitted, with restrictions
- Valet laundry service
- 1 restaurant; children's menu
- Indoor pool, sauna, exercise machines; some age restrictions

Westin Hotel Ottawa ✱ $$$

11 Colonel By Drive

Ottawa ON K1N 9H4

Tel 560-7000 or 1-800-228-3000

Fax 569-2013

Part of the Rideau Centre complex, which also includes

a large shopping mall and a convention centre, the Westin has one of the best views of Parliament Hill, the Rideau Canal, and the National War Memorial. Younger kids receive a special registration kit and gift when they check in.

- 484 rooms
- No CAA discount; children under 18 free; maximum 5 people per room
- Indoor valet parking; $19 per night; in-and-out privileges
- Minifridges; coffeemakers in 10 business rooms
- Cable TV; no VCR; pay TV
- Hairdryers
- Cribs, bottle-warmers, cots free
- Babysitting available
- 14 rooms provide disabled access, including roll-in showers; special equipment for hearing-impaired
- Non-smoking rooms
- Pets permitted, with restrictions
- Laundry service; dry cleaning service
- 1 restaurant; children's menu
- Indoor pool, sauna, fitness room, squash; children permitted with some restrictions

Hull

Holiday Inn Crowne Plaza Hull/Ottawa $$$

2 Montcalm Street
Hull QC J8X 4B4
Tel 819-778-3880 or
1-800-567-1962
Fax 819-778-3309

Close to the Canadian Museum of Civilization.

- 230 rooms; 12 suites
- CAA discount; children under 18 free
- Indoor parking; $9.25 per night; in-and-out privileges
- Minifridges in rooms; full kitchen in 1 suite; minifridges in 11 suites
- Cable TV; no VCR; pay TV
- Hairdryers
- Cribs free; cots $10
- Babysitting available
- Disabled access
- Non-smoking floors
- Pets permitted
- Valet laundry service
- 1 restaurant; children's menu; children under 18 eat free
- Indoor pool with lifeguard, sauna, whirlpool, exercise room

East of downtown

Chimo Hotel $

1199 Joseph Cyr
Gloucester ON K1J 7T4
Tel 744-1060 or 1-800-387-9779
Fax 744-7845

Close to National Museum of
Science and Technology.

- 230 rooms; 27 suites
- CAA discount; children
  under 18 free
- Free outdoor parking
- Minifridges in 173 rooms;
  coffeemakers in all rooms
- Suites have minifridges and
  coffeemakers; microwave
  available on request
- Cable TV; no VCR; pay TV
- Hairdryers in 30 rooms, all
  suites
- Cribs free; cots $15
- Limited disabled access
- Babysitting available
- Non-smoking floors
- Small pets permitted
- Valet laundry service
- 1 restaurant; children's
  menu
- Indoor pool, sauna,
  whirlpool; children under 16
  must be supervised

West of downtown

Best Western Macies Hotel $

1274 Carling Avenue
Ottawa ON K1Z 7K8
Tel 728-1951 or 1-800-268-5531
Fax 728-1955

Close to Westboro Village; 10
minutes by car to downtown.

- 115 rooms; 6 suites
- CAA discount; children
  under 14 free
- Free outdoor parking
- Refrigerators in 34 rooms
  and all suites
- Cable TV; no VCR; pay TV
- Hairdryers in some rooms
  and at front desk
- Cribs $9; cots $8
- Babysitting available
- Limited disabled access
- Non-smoking floors
- Pets permitted, with restric-
  tions
- Coin-op laundry
- 1 restaurant; children's
  menu
- Outdoor heated pool,
  sauna, whirlpool, health
  club; no children under 14,
  children over 13 must be
  supervised

The Talisman Hotel $$

1376 Carling Avenue
Ottawa ON K1Z 7L5
Tel 722-7600 or 1-800-267-4166
Fax 722-2226
Internet http://www.uplink/talisman

Close to Westboro Village; 10 minutes by car to downtown.

- 276 rooms; 12 suites
- CAA discount; children under 18 free
- Free outdoor parking
- Minifridges in 226 rooms; refrigerators or minifridges in suites
- Cable TV; no VCR; pay TV
- Hairdryers
- Cribs free; cots $10
- Babysitting available
- Limited disabled access
- Non-smoking floors
- No pets
- Valet laundry service
- 2 restaurants; children's menu
- 2 heated outdoor pools; children require supervision

South of downtown

Monterey Inn $$$

2259 Prince of Wales Drive
(Highway 16)

Ottawa ON K2E 6Z8
Tel 226-5813 or 1-800-565-1300
Fax 226-5900

Close to the Rideau River on the main southern access route; 10 minutes by car to downtown.

- 80 rooms; 7 suites
- CAA discount; children under 18 free
- Free outdoor parking
- No kitchen facilities in rooms; full kitchens in suites
- Cable TV; no VCR
- No hairdryers
- Cribs free; cots $8
- No babysitting available
- Disabled access
- Non-smoking rooms
- Pets permitted, $20
- Coin-op laundry
- 1 restaurant; discount for children
- Suites have access to sauna and whirlpool; outdoor pool; children require supervision

Suite hotels

Suite or apartment hotels have grown in popularity, thanks to the convenience they offer to visitors who are staying for more than just a couple of nights. Ottawa has a very large selection, because of the number of transient workers who visit the city on government business. Many of the rooms are occupied year-round by members of Parliament or their staff members, or by Armed Forces personnel stationed temporarily at National Defence Headquarters. For families who want to avoid the cost of eating out every day, a suite hotel with a kitchen could be ideal. Parking also tends to be cheaper than at regular hotels.

Albert at Bay Suite Hotel ✱ $$$

435 Albert Street
Ottawa ON K1R 7X4
Tel 238-8858 or 1-800-267-6644
Fax 238-1433
E-mail steph@igs.net

The western edge of Ottawa's core was the last to be developed, giving this modern suite-hotel complex a historic location, cheek by jowl with some of the city's older churches and the National Library and Archives of Canada. Parliament Hill is a 5-minute

Babysitting services

As much as we love them, we need to get away from our kids occasionally. There's no need to suffer guilt pangs; the kids feel the same way about us — especially when they're stuck with us on vacation. Most people have a network of part-time or full-time caregivers where they live; finding experienced, trustworthy help on the road so we can enjoy a meal alone or go out to a nightclub can be a challenge.

Most large hotels can arrange babysitting for guests through bonded local agencies, and will usually provide you with contact numbers so you can discuss your needs with the services yourself.

In Ottawa, there is another alternative if you need respite care for a morning or afternoon. Child Care Information, 235-7256, can arrange for short-term child supervision; it's best to give them as much advance notice as possible.

walk. On weekends, a free kids' club provides a supervised activity centre for children 3–12.

- 198 suites
- CAA discount; children under 16 free
- Underground parking; $8 per day, free to CAA members; in-and-out privileges
- Full kitchens
- Cable TV; no VCR; pay TV; video game rental
- Hairdryers
- Cribs and cots free
- Babysitting available
- Disabled access
- Non-smoking floors
- No pets
- Coin-op laundry; valet service
- 2 restaurants
- Sauna, whirlpool, fitness centre; children must be supervised

The Aristocrat Hotel $$

131 Cooper Street
Ottawa ON K2P 0E7
Tel 232-9471 or 1-800-563-5634
Fax 563-2836

Close to the Rideau Canal.

- 60 suites
- CAA discount; children under 16 free

- Free outdoor parking
- Full kitchens
- Cable TV; no VCR
- Cribs and cots free
- No babysitting available
- Disabled access
- Non-smoking rooms
- No pets
- Coin-op laundry; dry cleaning service
- 1 restaurant; children's menu
- Sauna, hot tub, weight room; children under 14 must be supervised

Arosa Apartment Hotel $

163 MacLaren Street
Ottawa ON K2P 2G4
Tel 238-6783
Fax 238-5080

Ten minutes from Parliament Hill.

- 61 suites
- CAA discount; full rates for children
- Indoor and outdoor parking; $4 per day; in-and-out privileges
- Full kitchens, including dishwashers
- Cable TV; no VCR
- No hairdryers
- Cribs $5 per day, $20 per week; high chairs free; no cots

- Babysitting available
- Limited disabled access
- Non-smoking rooms
- No pets
- Coin-op laundry; dry cleaning service
- Exercise facilities; children must be supervised

Best Western Victoria Park Suites $$

377 O'Connor Street
Ottawa ON K2P 2M2
Tel 567-7275 or 1-800-465-7275
Fax 567-1161

Close to the Canadian Museum of Nature.

- 100 suites
- CAA discount; children under 12 free
- Underground parking; $6 per day, free for CAA members; in-and-out privileges
- Full kitchens
- Cable TV; no VCR
- Hairdryers
- Cribs and high chairs free; no cots
- Babysitting available
- Limited disabled access
- Non-smoking floors
- No pets
- Laundry facilities
- No restaurant; free continental breakfasts
- Sauna and exercise

facilities; some restrictions on children

Cartier Place and Towers Suite Hotels $

180 Cooper Street
Ottawa ON K2P 2L5
Tel 236-5000 or 1-800-236-8399
Fax 238-3842

Ten minutes from Parliament Hill. Available free are a number of extras for children: strollers, Jolly Jumpers, children's life jackets, and bath toys.

- 202 suites; 4 rooms
- CAA discount; full rates for children
- Limited indoor parking; $7 per day; in-and-out privileges
- Full kitchens in suites; rooms have minifridges and coffeemakers
- Cable TV; VCR rental; pay TV; free cartoon channel
- Hairdryers
- Cribs $7.50; no cots
- Babysitting services
- Disabled access; 3 wheelchair-accessible suites
- Non-smoking floors
- No pets
- Coin-op laundry; valet service
- 1 restaurant; closed

Sundays

- Indoor pool, sauna, whirlpool, exercise room; children under 16 require supervision

Minto Place Suite Hotel ✸ $$$

433 Laurier Avenue West
Ottawa ON K1R 7Y1
Tel 232-2200 or 1-800-267-3377
Fax 232-6962

Built in the late 1980s, this hotel is several blocks southwest of Parliament Hill in a large complex of shops, restaurants, and banks. The hotel's Children's Club offers supervised, organized activities during summer months for children 4–12. Activities include arts, games, stories, excursions to Parliament and museums, films, and more, 9 am–noon and 1–4 pm. Evening sessions can be arranged on 24 hours' notice. Sessions cost $10 each, not including museum admissions and other incidental costs.

- 418 suites
- No CAA discount; children under 18 free
- Indoor parking; $10.44 per night; in-and-out privileges
- Full kitchens in 194 suites; kitchenettes in others
- Cable TV; no VCR; pay TV

- Hairdryers
- Cribs and high chairs free; no cots
- Babysitting services
- Disabled access; 2 suites specifically designed and equipped
- Non-smoking floors
- No pets
- Laundry service; dry cleaning service
- 2 restaurants; children's menus
- Indoor pool, sauna, whirlpool, fitness centre

Travelodge Hotel Ottawa by Parliament Hill ✸ $$

402 Queen Street
Ottawa ON K1R 5A7
Tel 236-1133 or 1-800-578-7878
Fax 236-2317

Five minutes from Parliament Hill.

- 175 suites
- CAA discount; children under 18 free
- Indoor parking; $8 per night; in-and-out privileges
- Full kitchens in 6 suites; kitchenettes in others
- Cable TV; no VCR; pay TV
- Hairdryers at front desk
- Cribs free; cots $10
- No babysitting available

- Disabled access, including some wheelchair-accessible suites
- Non-smoking floors
- Pets permitted, with restrictions
- Coin-op laundry; dry cleaning service
- 1 restaurant; children' menu
- Whirlpool; restricted to children over 15

University residences

In many cities, university residences offer budget alternatives to families travelling from May through August. In Ottawa, Carleton University offers the added bonus of one of the best locations in the city. Carleton's campus is bordered on one side by the Rideau Canal and well connected to downtown by bicycle and walking paths. Just across Hartwells Locks is the Dominion Arboretum and Botanic Garden, and beyond that the Central Experimental Farm. On another side of the university is Vincent Massey Park, a large urban park with many beautiful picnic spots, and the historic Glebe neighbourhood completes the

boundary. The rooms at the Carleton residence are typically spartan, but relatively modern. Summer residency gives guests access to the university's extensive recreational facilities, as well as its restaurants.

Carleton University Tour/ Conference Centre

1125 Colonel By Drive
Ottawa ON K1S 5B6
Tel 520-5611
Fax 520-3952

- 1000 rooms; $43 for 2 adjoining single rooms with shared bathroom and buffet breakfast; combinations of 3 or 4 adjoining rooms with common area also available
- Parking available at university's rates (varies at different lots)
- No kitchen facilities
- TV room on each floor; telephones in lobby
- Disabled access
- Air-conditioning; non-smoking rooms
- No pets
- Coin-op laundry
- Access to on-campus recreational and dining facilities at regular rates

Appendix 1 Emergency assistance

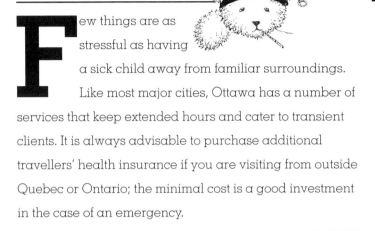

Few things are as stressful as having a sick child away from familiar surroundings. Like most major cities, Ottawa has a number of services that keep extended hours and cater to transient clients. It is always advisable to purchase additional travellers' health insurance if you are visiting from outside Quebec or Ontario; the minimal cost is a good investment in the case of an emergency.

If your child requires special medication, always take along sufficient amounts for your trip, as well as documentation from the child's physician in case you need to refill the prescription. It's always a good idea to put together your own first-aid kit, too, especially if you're travelling by car; these items can help you handle a health emergency until you can get help. Your needs may vary, but we usually take along:

- bandages, adhesive tape, disinfectant;
- some type of pain reliever;
- a thermometer;
- rubbing alcohol;
- Gravol for nausea and motion-sickness;
- sunscreen;
- medicated spray for relief from insect bites, minor skin abrasions, or sunburn;
- an antihistamine such as Benadryl for relief of allergic reaction.

Emergency Ambulance, Fire, and Police Services
Call 911
A 24-hour service. Your call will be directed to the appropriate agency.

161

After Hours Medical Clinics

1385 Bank Street, Suite 100

523-7440

117 Centrepointe Drive,
Suite 103, Nepean

228-2020

Walk-in medical clinics, operating outside normal office hours. Hours vary, but the clinics are generally open 7 days a week, 9 am–9 pm at Bank Street and 8 am–midnight in Nepean. Outside these hours, children exhibiting serious symptoms should be taken to the Children's Hospital of Eastern Ontario (see below) or to any other hospital emergency department.

Canadian Automobile Association (CAA) Emergency Road Service

820-1400

A 24-hour service for CAA and American Automobile Association members experiencing vehicle problems or in need of towing service.

Children's Hospital of Eastern Ontario (CHEO)

401 Smyth Road

737-7600 General switchboard

737-2328 Emergency

737-1100 Poison Control
Emergency Line

The best place to take children who have suffered serious accidents or are experiencing alarming symptoms. If your child's situation is not a genuine emergency, other options are available, such as a home visit or an after-hours clinic consultation. CHEO's emergency department is often very busy, and your wait could be long if your child's condition is not considered serious.

Dental Emergency Service

**Billings Bridge Plaza
  Shopping Centre**

**Riverside Drive and
  Bank Street**

737-4944

A 24-hour emergency dental service.

Distress Centre

238-3311

A 24-hour telephone counselling service for those experiencing emotional distress.

Medreach Physicians House Call Service

228-2020

Makes house calls after 5 pm on weeknights. From 8 am to midnight, 7 days a week, call ahead and you will be directed to a walk-in clinic.

Parent Preschool Resource Centre

300 Goulburn Crescent
565-2467

A drop-in centre for parents and their children, Mondays and Wednesdays 9 am–3 pm, Thursdays and Fridays 9 am–noon; Saturdays 9:30 am–noon. The centre's "Warm Line" (565-2467) operates Mondays–Fridays 1 pm–4 pm, offering parenting advice and information on children's activities and resources.

Poison Hotline

Children's Hospital of Eastern Ontario
737-1100

A 24-hour advice and assistance service, provided by the CHEO, that offers advice following accidental poisonings or suspected poisonings.

Shoppers Drug Mart

1460 Merivale Road, Nepean
224-7270

Open 24 hours for pharmacy and health-care products.

Veterinary Emergency Clinic

900 Boyd Avenue
725-1182
729-6139 Emergency Services

A 24-hour hospital, with veterinarian on premises during emergency hours.

Appendix 2
Free family fun

For a city that's taken more than its share of government cutbacks, Ottawa still offers a remarkable number of free attractions: landmarks like the Rideau Canal and Parliament Hill, national showcases like the National Gallery. Many more sights in the capital are free on specific days, or under certain conditions. And, of course, you can always enjoy the natural beauty of the city and its region at little or no cost in the many parks

Great attractions for free

Bank of Canada Currency Museum: Free admission on Tuesdays. See pages 68-69.

Bytown Museum: Free admission Sundays May 1 to Thanksgiving. See pages 69-70.

Canadian Museum of Civilization: Admission to the museum, including one of Ottawa's top attractions, the Children's Museum, is free on Sundays 9 am–noon. See pages 38-43.

Canadian Museum of Nature: Admission is free Thursdays after 5 pm and Canada Day. See pages 43-46.

Canadian War Museum: There is never a charge for Canadian veterans or their guests; admission for all is free Thursdays 5–8 pm. See pages 73-75.

National Aviation Museum: Admission to Canada's largest

collection of aircraft is free Thursdays 5–9 pm. See pages 49-51.

Other free attractions

Canadian Museum of Contemporary Photography: see pages 70-72.

Canadian Police College stables: see page 72.

Logan Hall/Geological Survey of Canada: see page 77.

National Gallery of Canada: permanent collection always free; children under 18 and full-time students can attend special exhibits free as well. See pages 52-54.

National Library and National Archives of Canada: see page 80.

Nepean Museum: see page 82.

Ottawa Art Gallery: see page 83.

Parliament Hill: see pages 58-62.

Pinhey's Point/Horaceville: see page 117. (Donations encouraged.)

Rideau Canal Skating: see pages 66-67. (Donations encouraged.)

Stittsville Flea Market: see page 117.

Wild Bird Care Centre: see pages 116-17. (Donations encouraged.

Free special events and performances

Aylmer Winter Carnival: see page 131.

Canada Day festivities on Parliament Hill: see page 134.

Canadian Police College (RCMP) Musical Ride: see page 72.

Canadian Tulip Festival (many free events, including the Tulip Flotilla): see page 132.

Christmas Lights Across Canada: see page 138.

Governor General's Levée: see page 130.

Ottawa International Jazz Festival (many free concerts): see page 134.

Ottawa Valley Book Festival (many free events): see page 131.

Remembrance Day: see page 138.

Winterlude: see pages 130-31.

Free tours

Ottawa International Hostel: see page 83.

Parliament Buildings: see pages 58-62.

Rideau Hall: see pages 83-84.

Photo credits

Binet, René/City of Gatineau: 137

Black, Garry/Masterfile: 7

Brooks, Bill/Masterfile: 120

Canadian Museum of Civilization: 39

Canadian Museum of Contemporary Photography: 71

Canadian Museum of Nature: 44, 46

Capital Trolley Tours: 89

Central Canada Exhibition Association: 135

Château Laurier: 146

City of Ottawa: 11, 37, 97, 102 bottom

City of Ottawa Archives: 22 (CA-0221)

Cumberland Township Museum: 112

Dobel, Mike/Masterfile: 60, 67, 102 top

Dubroy, Jason/OC Transpo: 32

Fisher, Larry/Masterfile: x

Harlequin Studios/Philip D. Owen, Director: 132

HCW Steam Train: 111

Kent, Bill: 74

Kraulis, J.A./Masterfile: 12, 42, 61

Lunn, S./Parks Canada: 13, 136

Morin, Brian/Parks Canada: 65, 76

National Aviation Museum: 51

National Capital Commission: 15 bottom, 30, 52, 59, 63, 78, 79, 109,   127, 131, 150, 152

National Film Board: 9

National Gallery of Canada: 53

National Museum of Science and Technology: 48, 55, 56, 57

Ottawa Lynx Baseball Club: 119

Ottawa Tourism and Convention Authority: 35, 98

Parks Canada: 15 top; 18, 19, 21, 70, 88

Piccadilly Bus Tours: 90

Rideau Valley Conservation Authority: 115

Roy, Sgt. Michel/Rideau Hall: 85 (GGC-95-472-10)

Royal Canadian Mounted Police: 73 (GRC 67-190-A)

Scouts Canada: 93

Sportfocus/OSHC Teckles/McElligott: 124

Transport Canada: 25, 26

Tunnels of Fun: 122

Veterans Affairs Canada: 81

Voyager Colonial Ltd.: 29

Index

James Hale and Joanne Milner met while they were both working for a city magazine in Ottawa. In the 18 years since then, James has pursued a career as a freelance travel writer, jazz critic, and corporate speechwriter. He is the author of *Branching Out: The History of the Royal Canadian Legion*. Joanne is a freelance researcher. They live in a village outside Ottawa with their two daughters. *Ottawa with Kids* is their first joint book.

Ottawa with Kids was designed and typeset by James Ireland Design Inc. The type is Memphis, a geometric slab serif, created in 1929 by Rudolf Weiss.

Illustrations by Pat Stephens
Maps by John Beaudry